MW00826301

Lubna,

The Angels brought you to me, this I know.

Thank you for being my Everything.

The Purpose

"Before we are individuals,
we are Beings built of emotion."

DEDICATION

To those who believe life is not to be wasted and that God doesn't grade on a curve.

The Purpose

I attest that everything in this book is true.

To protect the identities of those included in this book, I've changed only their names and certain details regarding their lives.

The details of my experiences have not been altered.

THE FIRST REALIZATION

Our Purpose is identifiable regardless
of where we exist in place or time.

The Purpose

I've always had a sense I've been here before.

For myself, there's never been any question that we are connected to a greater, permeating design.

I'm not psychic. I can't tell you if an aunt who has passed is standing next to you or if she has a message for you, but I have had psychic experiences.

Several.

The first occurred one November morning when I was fifteen years old. At that time, my family and I were living in Connecticut. I grew up in the southwestern corner of the state, a picturesque area of the country where ponds and small lakes dot a landscape of rolling hills, and each fall, Mother Nature worked her alchemic magic, breathing cold air through the leafy green canopies of summer, transforming them into fiery tapestries of red, orange, and gold.

At this time of year, I was filling out job applications for the coming summer.

The Purpose

I wanted to be a lifeguard, but the competition was tough. To get a job, one had to apply months in advance in the hopes of grabbing an opening created by a departing senior or a college student who was moving on to the world of full-time work.

That morning, I awoke having been shaken by a dream. The dream wasn't ominous, nor was it some foreboding nightmare. Oddly, the dream was a vision of a woman standing in front of me with tennis courts behind her. She was athletic, in her late thirties to early forties, and her blond hair was tied in a ponytail. She wore a white tennis dress and held a racquet in her left hand. The image was the opposite of terrifying, but what the woman did shook me.

She called me by name.

She knew who I was, and somehow, I knew, in a way that I can't explain, that I was supposed to know who she was. However, I had never seen the woman before. She was a complete stranger to me. Yet her familiarity with me, and the penetrating sense that I was supposed to recognize her, was so strong I awoke in a sweat.

Late that following January, I received the replies from the lifeguarding applications I had submitted. No luck.

The Purpose

All the lifeguards from the preceding summer were returning. However, several weeks later in February, I received a phone call from the parks department in town. They asked if I'd be interested in working at their tennis courts instead of as a lifeguard. Lacking any other prospects, I accepted.

Halfway through the summer, sitting in the pro shop, I was looking at the court reservation schedule when someone called my name. I turned to look and there was *the exact vision* from my dream several months earlier. There stood Mrs. Williamson, a regular player, with the tennis courts behind her, *precisely* as I had seen that one November morning. I almost fell over. Apparently, at least some of the color left my face because she asked if I was all right. I assured her I was fine, physically at least.

At that point in the summer, I knew exactly who she was and I was completely familiar with her. She played tennis every week.

How was that possible?

How could I have seen an image at a time in my life when all of my conscious thoughts were about being a lifeguard and I had no knowledge of the tennis courts conjured in my dream? *I had never even been* in the pro shop at which I ended up working. On that November morning, I didn't even know the job I ended up with existed, much less that Mrs. Williamson existed. I had never seen her before.

As my life went on, it turned out this wouldn't be my only supernatural experience. The next one would occur a number of years later when I was returning home from college. I was in my senior year, and it was quite common for me to return from school periodically, meeting my parents at the airport and spending a few days visiting friends and family. However, for some reason, this trip was different.

After the plane landed and taxied toward the gate, I reached down to pull my backpack out from beneath the seat in front of me. At that moment, it was as though a female voice whispered in my ear, "Your parents didn't come to get you. Your friends are here."

I shot straight up in my seat and looked over my right shoulder expecting to see someone, but no one was there. As I exited the plane, I walked into the gate area to discover two of my closest friends who, wanting to surprise me, had called my parents asking if they could pick me up at the airport. When I got home that night, my mom asked me if I was shocked to see them. I told her, "Well, you're not going to believe this."

I would go on to have several more clairaudient experiences and one clairvoyant experience in my life. They were different than my first dream experience, and I learned that these later occurrences would always share two characteristics: 1) they were concise (I would often joke that it was as if the senders were being charged by the word, as the messages were constructed in the shortest manner possible to convey the intended meaning), and 2) their messages always related to those who were close to me, those whom I loved.

Although I was surprised when any of them happened, their existence and their illustration that, in some way, we are all connected wasn't surprising. I simply found it surprising that these events were happening to *me*. For myself, it was understandable that they would occur, as I never questioned whether each of us is part of an encompassing, eternal design. My questions have always been: "How are we connected?" and "Why are we here?"

What awaits us after this life, and are we supposed to do something while we're here to prepare for it? Are our lives comprised of repeated journeys, and if so, why would a person have lived here before? Why would they come back? On the other hand, why would a person only live once? And, perhaps most importantly, how does it all work?

I didn't know the answers to these questions, but I wanted to. Regrettably, I discovered my curiosity and best intentions didn't entitle me to some divine insight. Instead, if I wanted the answers, I was going to have to uncover them on my own—but I didn't know how.

It took me several years of pursuing, plodding down, and giving up on several different paths before discovering the right one. Frustratingly, in hindsight, I realized it had all been embarrassingly simple.

If we are all part of a universal design, one in which we are connected, that design must leave an identifiable, transcendent fingerprint revealing itself, as it can't exist in just one person, in one group of people, or in one moment in time. It has to exist within *all people throughout all of time.*

I needed to find a *constant* hiding amongst us, connecting us all—one that crossed the boundaries of time, culture, geography, age, gender, education level, income level, and religion. Whatever it was, it couldn't be something subjective or prescriptive that changes with the whims of varying cultures or individual personalities. Instead, it has to permeate every person around the world, so each can discover on his or her own answers to life's most important questions.

As I would discover, only one thing possesses all of these traits and, in the course of finding it, I uncovered our Purpose.

How could I have known that one, inconceivably simple, self-evident thing would explain everything?

Turning Away

What I was taught growing up didn't make sense to me.

I had always held an unshakable belief in God and never doubted that a higher power exists. I had always *felt* it. Yet, with equal conviction, I also believed God isn't discriminatory, and in fact, is the exact opposite: an all-accepting Being of pure love. That's why what I was taught didn't make sense.

The concept of an absolute Heaven and Hell seemed discriminatory. Those who believed and followed the "right" path had an opportunity to get in; those who didn't wouldn't.

How was that consistent with the existence of an all-loving Being? Further, what happens to those who are never formally taught about the existence of Heaven, Hell, and their associated "right" and "wrong" ways to live? Are they automatically eliminated from consideration for eternal bliss?

More specifically, what are the precise criteria for realizing either Heaven or Hell? Where are those rules spelled out *universally* for *everyone* to understand? Shouldn't each of us be issued the same guidebook upon arrival, or something? Or shouldn't we at least get a practice quiz before taking the final exam?

What if I live to be one hundred years old, and for the first ninety-nine years, I live a life that puts me on a path to eternal bliss, but in the last year of my life, I make a mistake? Will I be condemned to eternal damnation for that one mistake?

Or, what if the opposite were true? What if I'm born into a life of hardship, one in which I struggle to survive, stealing to stay warm, but after a youth of hardship, I become highly successful, building hospitals, charities, and schools that continue to help others long after I am gone? Will I be condemned for all eternity for the transgressions in my youth? Even though I spent the majority of my life contributing to the betterment of others?

The Purpose

How could an all-loving Being create a discriminatory afterlife? It didn't seem fair, just, or right.

I believed there had to be another explanation, but eschewing my religious upbringing wasn't something I took lightly. Although I wanted to steer my life down a different path that I believed would make more sense, I was also scared. For one thing, I didn't know where to turn.

What was I pursuing? What if my instincts were nothing more than transient feelings, and the cost of listening to them was eternal damnation?

Based on everything I had been taught, there wasn't any room for error. It was either up or down, and quite frankly, I was afraid of being wrong. Selfishly, I had no desire to spend all of eternity in Hell.

Yet, despite the potential consequences, some immovable force within refused to let me embrace the teachings of my youth. As much as I would try, it just wasn't possible. Fearful, at age sixteen I turned away from everything I was taught was right and moved toward an ambiguous, instinctual hope—one that I felt somehow contained new understanding and awareness.

It would prove to be the greatest decision of my life.

It would also teach me that in order to see what is here, we have to alter our perspective and shed a number of perceptions, no matter how deeply ingrained they might be.

* * * * * * * * * *

My First Clue: Transcendence

I was one of the lucky ones.

My parents provided me with a fortuitous life. Although retired now, they were hardworking people who started with very little and acquired everything they had through sheer will, the power of their dreams, determination, and, for my father, virtually tireless labor. Accordingly, they gave to me an appreciation for hard work and responsibility.

They weren't physically or emotionally abusive. They didn't use drugs. They were able to give me the benefits of a stay-at-home mom, and they gave back to the community (and still do) by volunteering their time, making charitable donations, and providing resources to individuals in need. They also provided me with another gift: exposure, by choosing to show my sister and me different cultures, people, events, and countries.

It was also when I was sixteen that we took our first trip to Europe. We traveled to London and Paris, staying for a few days in each city and seeing their famous landmarks. Unknowingly, this trip provided the foundation of the journey I had chosen to take, for although it happened unexpectedly, it was the first time I saw the unmistakable, transcendent elements that exist within us.

Even though the US and the UK are alike in many ways, they also have a number of distinctly different customs and expressions. In fact, I was surprised by how difficult it was at times to understand "English," recognizing for the first time what was meant by the expression "two people separated by a common language."

In comparison, France was truly foreign. Although I had studied the language, my understanding was rudimentary, and I felt intimidated when attempting anything beyond ordering chicken on a menu or buying train tickets.

In the end, however, it was this detachment from my own familiarity that allowed me to see more clearly. Unable to speak their language fully, I was reduced to understanding what people showed me through their expressions. Laughs, smiles, tears, wrinkled brows of confusion, eye rolls of frustration, and sighs of impatience were all "words" I understood these "foreign people" to be "speaking."

At their intangible, emotional core, these people shared with me an unspoken language that I knew instinctively, one in which I was completely fluent. This universal, common language provided my first clue.

As I grew older and continued to travel, my observations became more detailed. Compiling those details revealed an unmistakable conclusion: life points in a specific direction, one that illuminates an identifiable Purpose that is benevolent and just and can be discovered by anyone in a single lifetime regardless of their age, income level, education level, race, gender, geographical location, or place in time.

I also learned that this Purpose is rooted in the only thing that remains constant throughout all human history, the same thing I saw on my first trip to Europe: the design behind our emotions.

* * * * * * * * * *

THE SECOND REALIZATION

Emotion drives all human behavior.

THE THIRD REALIZATION

Emotion is not only transcendent but directional in its nature,
and its direction reveals our Purpose.

* * * * * * * * *

"Now I am not one of the most constant creatures alive myself, and
am apt to run through the spectrum which has the blues at the
bottom about once a week."

—Byron Caldwell Smith (1849—1877),
letter to Kate Stephens

"Emotion always has its roots in the unconscious and manifests
itself in the body."
—Irene Claremont de Castillejo

* * * * * * * * *

My Second Clue: Design and Direction

The range of human emotions

Hate   **Love**

Anchored on one end by love, at the other by hate, and containing a myriad of feelings in between, each of us has a range of emotions within us. For all the rational, logical thought of which we're capable, we are Beings driven and influenced by the emotions within our cores. *Everything* we do is powered by emotion.

In the course of our evolution, our emotions evolved before the parts of our brains responsible for rational thought. Physiologically, our emotions provide a foundation that triggers our feelings and underlies the thoughts we create.[1]

In this regard, conscious thought channels our underlying, driving emotions into behaviors (e.g., going to work creates financial security for ourselves; by socializing with others we feel acceptance and belonging). More significantly, aside from being at

---

[1] Mary Lamia, Ph.D., "Like It Or Not, Emotions Will Drive the Decisions You Make Today," *Psychology Today*, December 21, 2010.

the center of everything, emotion also transcends the physical boundaries of our bodies.

Without touching us physically, even from a distance, others can change our emotional states (and therefore perhaps ourselves) simply by expressing their own emotions. For example, a funny actor can make us happy, and a dictator or tyrant can make us mad or fearful; both can achieve this through playful antics or angry scowls and without saying a word. Seemingly, we communicate and exchange our emotions with others invisibly, transcendentally, and instantly.

Sherrie Bourg Carter, Psy.D., details the phenomena of Emotional Contagion (EC) in which both good and bad emotions influence those in proximity to the "host." Her research has shown good emotions such as happiness "spread through social networks, much like a virus." Of course, this also holds true with negative or bad emotions like depression, where "one family member's depression can bring down an entire family system."[2]

Nothing else has this power. Why do emotions?

---

[2] Sherrie Bourg Carter, Psy.D., "Emotions Are Contagious—Choose Your Company Wisely," *Psychology Today*, October 12, 2012.

The Purpose

After all, aren't we just mortal beings here to eat, sleep, make money, and live before passing on? Why does some ageless, invisible force drive all of our behaviors? And how exactly is it connected to us? After all, we're not born with "young" compassion, nor do we grow "old" compassion as we age. We only have young bodies and old bodies, not emotions.

When we want to gain or lose weight, we don't say: "I think I'm going to gain or lose a couple of pounds of envy." Instead, from the day we are born, we are imbued with a variety of feelings, such as joy, sadness, anger, disgust, frustration, and happiness, and the capacity for these feelings remains within each of us for our entire lives, no matter who we are or where we are in the world.

Why are we designed that way? More importantly, these forces are doing more than drive us, because it turns out, they're pointing us in a specific direction.

But where, and more importantly, why?

Love

I have known its magic only once.

The Purpose

Although my family provided a foundation of love upon which my life has been built, I have known the fulfillment that comes from finding the one who is my Everything in only one person. Fortunately, she is with me now, and with her, I am rich, as every day she gives me a thousand different gifts that I would never receive otherwise.

It took me a long time to find my "exceptional half." I say that because she is far more than my "better half." One day, before our paths crossed, I was told she was coming, but I had no idea when we would meet. This time, my experience wasn't a whisper of a woman's voice, nor was it a dream in which someone appeared. It was a "knowing," an unquestionable awareness, as though something was telling me from within that she was near, and my time searching was coming to an end.

The day it happened, my mind was occupied completing routine tasks around the house. Yet there it was, interrupting, intruding, and telling me. I knew I would find her soon but had no idea when, where, or even who she would be.

When it happened, it did so through a chance meeting with friends at a restaurant. On the surface, it was nothing more than a random encounter resulting from one of my close friends running into Lubna's friend.

The Purpose

The two of them said "hello" and started catching up with one another, which left Lubna and I standing there, somewhat awkwardly. She was tall and beautiful and greeted me with a warm, welcoming smile. We started talking and I found her friendly and witty. In a fateful alignment of time, place, and spirit, we began what would prove to be the entwining of two souls.

Today, she is my true love, the one without whom my life would be forever and irreparably less. She later told me that on the night we met, she had a feeling, one that compelled her to convince her friend to go to that particular restaurant, but she did not know why. Her impulse forever changed both of our lives.

Now, with her, I am never alone. Even when we are separated physically, what I used to know as loneliness has been replaced with longing. Having come together, I am undoubtedly more than who I otherwise am.

Today, I am healthier.

Yet I didn't do anything to change. The only change that happened in my life was external to me. Someone who entered my life was now alighting my senses, touching me, loving me, and somehow, as a result, I have become stronger, happier, and content.

The Purpose

Although there were fun things I would do in my life prior to the two of us meeting, inside, they were never as fulfilling as they are now. To be honest, previously, there were times in which I had known a pronounced emptiness, one that enables me to appreciate all the more the gift I have today.

Like many, I had dated both casually and seriously, knowing the fun that would come with meeting someone new, but also the pain that could come with loss or rejection, even when it was clear to both of us things weren't meant to be. Little did I know then that the emotions associated with separation cause a pain that is measurable.

Research has shown that the pain felt during periods of loss or breakup registers in the brain the same way as physical pain. "When someone feels physical pain, opioids are released in the brain so that the significance of the pain is inhibited. We now know this same experience occurs when an individual feels slighted or rejected by others," according to Nicole Fisher, an expert on brain health and president of Health and Human Rights Strategies.

Fisher goes on to state, "the pain of rejection can reduce one's reasoning ability by 30% and IQ by up to 25%."[3] Clearly, our emotions are connected to our bodies in ways in which the absence or withdrawal of love causes profound and detrimental changes to our physiology.

Conversely, "falling in love causes our body to release a flood of feel good chemicals. Levels of these substances, which include dopamine, adrenaline, and norepinephrine, increase when two people fall in love,"[4] creating positive changes within us.

Underscoring this idea further, the negative health effects of loneliness or the absence of love and acceptance are many: "Individuals with less social connection have disrupted sleep patterns, altered immune systems, more inflammation and higher levels of stress hormones. One recent study found that isolation increases the risk of heart disease by twenty-nine percent and stroke by thirty-two percent."

---

[3] Nicole Fisher, "Rejection and Pain Are the Same to Your Brain," *Forbes*, December 25, 2015.

[4] From materials provided by Loyola University Health System. "What falling in love does to your heart and brain," *ScienceDaily*, February 6, 2014.

Another analysis that pooled data from seventy studies and 3.4 million people found that "socially isolated individuals had a thirty percent higher risk of dying in the next seven years and that this effect was largest in middle age."[5]

Yikes! All of these physical issues and benefits from having or lacking certain emotions, feelings, and social connections?

Yes.

What in the world is going on here?

Why are we designed so that *we experience physical consequences* when love is absent and we feel *a flood of positive benefits* when love is present? What is life trying to teach us?

Often, when people contemplate why we're here, they say, "We're here to love." Of course, given the above, that would seem a straightforward conclusion. However, if that were true, it would ignore all of our other emotions, making them meaningless.

---

[5] Dhruv Kuller, "How Social Isolation Is Killing Us," *New York Times*, December 22, 2016.

The Purpose

Although love is clearly important in our lives, our Purpose ends up being about more than love alone. Discovering our Purpose requires us to understand *all* of who we are, and we do this by acquiring one attribute in particular.

Combined with love, that one attribute then reveals why we are here.

* * * * * * * * *

THE FOURTH REALIZATION
We are born from, and remain connected to,
the universe, and its Purpose permeates us.

* * * * * * * * *

"As far as we can discern, the sole purpose of human existence is to kindle a light in the darkness of mere being. It may even be assumed that just as the unconscious affects us, the increase in our consciousness affects the unconsciousness."
—*Carl Gustav Jung*

The Purpose

My Third Clue: Perspective

Rafting through red canyons on the Colorado River out of Moab, Utah, proved to be the most relaxing trip I had ever taken. I was without phone service for five days, and the trip was a complete disconnect from the office. It was the first time I hadn't taken work with me. From that point on, I would try to do the same on all future vacations.

Stumbling upon two-day-old cougar prints, navigating roiling whitewater, sharing stories around crackling fires, showering beneath natural waterfalls, and even playing a makeshift game of beach volleyball on a sandbar punctuated several days of getting away. In the evenings, after the storytelling had died down and the quiet settled in, the night would come alive, shooting meteors across her sky, unleashing the brilliance of her moon, and casting thousands of stars across her inky black curtain, all of which presented more puzzles.

Lying beneath the night sky, I peered into a universe estimated to be fourteen billion years old. Of course, as humans, we only live approximately one hundred years, and that was what I found puzzling.

The Purpose

Why would we only live one hundred years in a world that has lived fourteen billion? Why would our Purpose be found here, in a lifetime that, in comparison, is infinitesimally short, rather than being part of a fourteen-billion-year existence? Or, was I looking at it from the wrong perspective?

Are we extensions of the universe that surrounds us? Given that we are literally made of the stuff that created the stars and planets (according to the Big Bang theory), do celestial connections remain between the stars and ourselves? If so, how?

Stargazing along the river those several nights, I realized that whatever Purpose exists for us here has to connect to what exists out there. It has to provide a bridge linking one hundred years with fourteen billion. After all, universal and transcendent can't just mean universal here on earth.

It has to mean *universal.*

It was then that I knew. I had been looking at our lives here—our world—as being the center of our Purpose. I had to invert my life view and see our world from whence it came, its source: the stars encompassing us.

The Purpose

It was similar to viewing a large mural, one that was ten feet tall and forty feet long. In this example, our lives are just one element in the mural.

If I stand close to the mural, I can see my daily activities: going to work, paying bills, working around the house, etc.: the things I do to ensure my physical survival. Near the mural, I can see the things I experience every day. That was the perspective I had seen throughout my life: the Near Perspective—the one that showed what was in front of me but not the all-encompassing picture in which our lives exist.

I was missing the rest of the mural. I lacked the Distant Perspective, revealed only by stepping back from my daily routines to see the mural in its entirety, where the message the painter created, the one connecting everything, exists.

Somehow, I had to change my perspective, but I didn't yet know how.

After returning to work, the stress created by the frenetic pace of striving to create a better and more comfortable life for myself came back. Within forty-eight hours, I experienced another disconnect. This one from the relaxing and restorative pace of life I had known for several days while on the river.

The Purpose

I've always been a daydreamer, and that didn't change simply by being at work. While at my desk, I fantasized about living full-time the relaxing life I had experienced while I was away. If only I didn't have to work. If only I was financially secure and could afford everything I needed. Then, I would be at rest.

Right?

As my dreams wandered, and visions of financial abundance consumed my thoughts, I was surprised to admit to myself that even if I had all the material things I needed to survive, I wouldn't be fulfilled. There would be something within me that would yearn for more. Not physical things. Intangible things. Some force within would still drive me to fulfill needs that can't be sated financially.

I would seek love to realize life's deepest gift, but I would also be driven by curiosity to explore new things. I would gravitate toward having fun and laughing with my friends over a good meal, which in turn would provide social gratification and the inner warmth that comes with it.

But if I wanted to buy those things, how much would they cost? What is the going rate for love, knowledge, and laughter among friends, even with all the money in the world?

The Purpose

It was then I knew that I had found my next clue. For some deliberate reason, we have to fulfill more than the physical needs required to sustain us every day.

My meandering mind had unwittingly showed me that what I was missing resides right inside each of us, in the only part of ourselves that, like the universe surrounding us, is timeless. We are not comprised solely of our physical existence, but rather the combination of our physical and emotional existence. It's as though we're comprised of two selves, each with its own needs, and to be completely healthy, we have to nourish and develop *both*.

What I hadn't yet discovered was what did our "emotional self" look like? What needs does it have, and just as importantly, why does it exist? Before my journey was complete, I would discover the answers to these questions.

I would also discover that the emotional dimension of ourselves connects us to far more than I ever knew—the Distant Perspective of life's mural—that I had yet to see.

* * * * * * * * *

The Purpose

"All learning has an emotional base."

—Plato

* * * * * * * * * *

Growing Up

In high school, I was fortunate to have a wonderful circle of friends. They were funny, colorful, bright, and gifted in so many varying ways that, arguably, I learned more about life and living from them than I did from my formal curriculum.

Of course, we had the usual growth pangs associated with coming-of-age teenagers: disagreements over things that seemed important at the time, petty rivalries, and occasional jealousies around dating and who was going with whom to school dances, all of which still punctuate my memories of the times, but we also grew. I learned much from them and recall hoping even then that I offered them as much in return.

A number of my friends were gifted intellectually. They could readily grasp advanced concepts in calculus and physics that, to me, were—and largely still are—quite foreign. Although later in life I would take a test that measured my IQ to be genius level, whatever intelligence I have is not wired naturally to digest what my friends were able to absorb so easily.

Yet if someone was having a problem or if they were troubled emotionally, I seemed to sense it from afar and/or earlier than most. I also seemed to understand intuitively and quickly what was needed for resolution. Although I might not have been able to tutor my friends in either math or science, it seemed I was able to offer advice and solve problems even for those more academically able than myself, which struck me as odd.

Why was I able to sense certain things more readily or further away than some? Particularly given the intellectual gifts others possessed?

It was at this point in my life that I believed different types of intelligence exist. In high school, we talked about people having "book smarts" and others who had "street smarts." I always felt I was in the latter category.

However, a few years after I graduated college, I walked into a bookstore. On the table of current bestsellers, I understood immediately that another more specific definition existed for what I had observed in high school. *Emotional Intelligence: Why*

It Can Matter More Than IQ, by Daniel Goleman, had just come out and was displayed prominently.

As soon as I read the title, I knew that's what I had. I picked it up immediately and leafed through it hungrily. The several things I read all resonated within, and I bought the book on the spot to take home in the hopes that I might understand more about myself.

I did.

I learned that, among other things, people with a high "Emotional Quotient" (EQ) could walk into a crowded room and recognize who designed the centerpiece on the table. Although I hadn't experienced that specific situation, I understood precisely what Goleman was saying.

At that point in my life, I was aware that, for some reason, subconsciously, my mind catalogued and correlated emotional and physical cues others expressed, creating an "emotional fingerprint," so that when I encountered those same cues again I would immediately conjure the profile of the personality behind them. For example, on several occasions after college, after talking to someone for only a few minutes and/or noting how they were dressed and carried themselves, I could tell them things such as:

the work they do (in one case, describing to someone the type of art she created and the medium she used most often), how many siblings they have, whether their siblings were older or younger, if their siblings were brothers or sisters, and approximately how far apart they were in age.

For those I met, the effect must've appeared somewhat psychic. In reality, it was anything but. It was nothing more than the result of a cataloguing process in which, for some reason, my brain had been engaged my entire life. When someone triggered enough cues, which often took only a few minutes, I was able to recall a profile I had seen previously.

Other traits of high-EQ individuals include patience and delayed gratification, understanding one's emotions and the emotional states of others, and exhibiting high levels of empathy.[6] These were all things I recognized readily.

What wasn't obvious was why do we have a specific form of intelligence designed to help us understand our emotional states and those of the people around us? The reason for IQ is clear.

---

[6] Daniel Goleman, *Emotional Intelligence: Why It Matters More Than IQ* (Bantam Books, 1995).

IQ is what we use to solve problems, find and cook food, analyze data, design new products, pay bills, run financial models for businesses, understand and sign mortgages, etc. It's a tool to ensure our physical survival.

But why do we have EQ? What is so critical about our emotional survival that we have a specific and separate type of intelligence to address it? Why are there two systems of intelligence within each of us?

Drifting back to my time lying beneath the star-filled darkness along the Colorado River reminded me that somehow, our lives here had to connect with everything out there. Clearly, any connection to the stars we have must exist in something that permeates us rather than being confined to the physical limits of our bodies. At this point, there was only one part of us that fits that definition.

* * * * * * * * *

THE FIFTH REALIZATION
The quality of our physical lives and the extent of our emotional growth are directly related to the choices we make managing our emotional selves.

THE SIXTH REALIZATION

Everything about an individual's character, path, and place in the universe can be defined by recognizing the extent to which he or she embraces or rejects specific core emotions.

* * * * * * * * *

"Feelings are much like waves, we can't stop them from coming but we can choose which one to surf."
—Jonatan Mårtensson

* * * * * * * * *

My Awakening

It was so simple, and it had been right in front of me my entire life.

We're taught everything growing up: what to eat, how to dress, read, write, everything. Yet we're never taught how to laugh, cry, express happiness, anger, joy, etc. We're never taught these *universal forms of communication*, because it's not necessary.

They're built into us.

The Purpose

We arrive here with the knowledge and ability to communicate with anyone anywhere in the world, and this has been true throughout the entire course of human existence. Emotional intelligence is embedded within us by life, the universe, our greater design, from wherever it is from which we come. It's the component within ourselves that *transcends everything*.

In that regard, *we* are universal.

That was my Awakening, my epiphany, my "aha" moment, in which things started coming into focus; but what is so important about emotional intelligence that it is built into all of us as well as everyone who has ever lived? Why are we emotional Beings at our core? What are we meant to do with this ability?

IQ is also given to us, but it doesn't transcend. If it did, we wouldn't need to be taught everything to survive. Instead, it's what we use to learn, understand, and provide for ourselves while we are here.

We are built with a duality comprised of our physical, finite selves, governed by IQ, and our emotional selves, which is governed by a timeless and universally present emotional intelligence. This I now understood.

The Purpose

What I didn't know was that the most extraordinary experience in my life was about to happen next, one that, ultimately, would show me how everything works.

Helping a friend

I was living in Texas when I discovered Daniel Goleman's book. At that time, I had a circle of friends with whom I'd get together for BBQs, go out in the evenings, enjoy Super Bowl parties, and do the things circles of friends do.

Susan was one of the funniest people in the group. She had a comical energy that blended witty one-liners with surprising antics, such as coming out of a restaurant bathroom with a long trail of toilet paper deliberately stuck inside her pants and dragging ten or so feet behind her for everyone to see. She injected an entertaining spontaneity that was hard to replicate and which always made her welcome at parties.

I don't recall how long Susan had been married, but it had been long enough to have two young boys, aged seven and four. Nor do I know what led her to make a change, but at some point, she decided she and her two boys would be better off alone. She chose to get a divorce, even though it meant taking on one of the toughest jobs known to humankind: a working single mother.

Unafraid of what might await her, she was happy about her decision and carried on as she always had, but now she was celebrating the brighter future she believed lay ahead. Of course, her happiness was contagious, affecting the rest of us whenever we would get together to provide the social connections each of us needed in our own ways.

About a year after Susan's divorce, her mom received a dreaded diagnosis: liver cancer. Worse, it had progressed extensively, and her prognosis was bleak.

Susan's mom lived on the East Coast, approximately 1,500 miles away, and Susan was the only person who could assist her. Unbeknownst to myself, at the time of her mom's diagnosis, Susan had been falling behind at her job.

She was bringing work home with her every night and weekend to keep up, but was still unable to get on top of it, creating concerns for her as to whether or not she'd keep her job. Combined with the needs of her two boys and ailing mom, Susan's infectious happiness yielded slowly to the worry and burden that comes with financial and medical uncertainty.

Of course, there's never a good time for anyone to receive a cancer diagnosis, but being spread as thinly as she already was, it would be hard to imagine a worse time for Susan to have received her mom's news. Now, on top of trying to balance everything at home, for an unknown period of time, she would have to travel east every weekend to help her mom fight her grave battle and mounting medical bills.

I don't know the specifics about her weekends back east. What I do know is that the doctors employed experimental treatments on Susan's mom, attempting to do everything they could to try to save her life. Unfortunately, at least a few of those experimental treatments had side effects, some of them painful.

For Susan, like so many others whose families battle with cancer, it was an emotional roller coaster. Some weeks her mom seemed to improve. During others, she clearly regressed and suffered.

As the weeks continued, the strain mounted. The medical bills, travel expenses, concerns about her job, and two boys who desperately needed their mother were all stretching Susan to a breaking point. Despite some periodic good news about her mom, overall, it seemed like Susan's mother was steadily slipping away. On the rare occasions when we were around Susan, Susan's condition seemed to be deteriorating as well.

The Purpose

No longer was she filled with unexpected antics or witty one-liners. Rather than seeing the fun-loving light in her eyes that had been so prevalent, her eyes were now distant and withdrawn as though they were preoccupied elsewhere. It was clear she was in need of help.

As she shared more details with us, I realized with regret that there wasn't much I could do. I couldn't help with her work at the office, and there certainly wasn't anything I could do to help her mom. Being active in Big Brothers and Sisters at the time, I knew that spending time with boys when their parents were absent or unable to makes a difference. It was the only way I thought I could help.

I had met her boys before, as Susan had brought them to some of our backyard barbeques. Lacking anything else, I offered to come by for a couple of evenings to play ball with the boys, bring pizza, etc. At a minimum, I thought it might give Susan some uninterrupted time to focus on her work.

For two or three weeks, once or twice a week, I would go over to their house and do simple things that boys like to do such as throw the ball around in the backyard, play with their toys, be superheroes, etc. My contributions were little things, not any one of them significant.

However, as time went on, the boys would get excited when they knew I was coming over. Perhaps they looked forward to those times together because of the things we did, or, more likely, because those times provided a brief escape from what I later understood to be the contagion of worry and distress growing within their home, emotional burdens that are felt by even the youngest child.

One night when I was about to leave, Susan made a comment. She said she didn't think she could take anymore. She was stressed, frustrated, and said she was "just going to take a pill" to end her troubles.

Although it was a comment that could hold the direst consequences, she said it so matter-of-factly and even a bit flippantly that I didn't take it seriously. She wasn't emotional, nor did she appear as though she didn't have any fight left.

The Purpose

Given her nature for joking around, I thought it was just an off-the-cuff comment and a way for her to vent. Believing she was just talking in the moment, I replied a bit matter-of-factly.

"You're not going to do that. You have your boys, and all of this is temporary. Everything will pass," I said, and that was pretty much it. She didn't mention anything else about it that night. We talked a bit more, and then I left.

The next time I went over to see the boys, again she mentioned she was "going to take a pill" to end her troubles. Again, her tone was more matter-of-fact than distressed.

Once more, I told her "you're not going to do that," and tried to assure her all of this was temporary. However, unlike the previous night, this time, she was defiant.

"I am," she said.

Although I'm certainly not an expert in recognizing people who are suicidal, even in her defiance, I didn't feel as though the situation that evening was critical, just a bit more serious than the previous night. A few months later, I would discover how wrong I was and in a way that I never could've imagined.

The Purpose

That evening, we talked for a while longer. I told her that no matter how formidable all the challenges may seem, things would resolve themselves, and she and the boys would be all right. She mentioned the mounting bills, financial pressure, uncertainty about her job, and, of course, the emotional ups and downs with her mom.

I tried to find the best words I could, and, to this day, I'm unsure as to whether I succeeded. Although I didn't think there was imminent danger, something within me made me feel it'd be best if I stayed on their sofa that night.

For some reason, we can find comfort and reassurance knowing someone else is in the house with us. So, that evening I stayed, and the next morning, when Susan got up, I left, and she never mentioned taking a pill again. She didn't have to, because shortly thereafter, everything changed.

Two days later, Susan received the news she had been dreading. Her mom had passed. Of course, we never want to lose loved ones, but sometimes one's passing can be more of a blessing than a curse. Given her mom's suffering, I felt that was the case here.

The Purpose

I honestly don't recall how often I went over to see the boys after her mom passed. I know it wasn't a lot, as the mood in the house shifted noticeably. With her mom's passing, Susan's roller coaster ride had ended.

Susan was able to grieve, and, in so doing, she pulled her boys closer to her. The feelings of distress abated. In time, she was able to focus on her work and what was ahead rather than the uncertainty that came with each day.

Her energy changed. She ended up keeping her job. She and her boys returned to the playful times they had always known. Their troubles passed, and things returned to normal for the three of them.

Life went on with our circle of friends, and, as she had done before, on occasion, Susan would bring the boys around. From time to time, Susan would talk about losing her mom.

With all the energy she expended to be by her side, I was surprised to learn the two of them weren't close. In fact, based on what she shared with me, I would describe their relationship as estranged.

The Purpose

Of course, no parent is perfect, but at a minimum we hope they'll be supportive and nurturing. Although Susan's mom wasn't abusive, from the stories Susan shared, it sounded as though alienating and occasionally demeaning could be accurate descriptors for her.

Of course, when she discussed her mom, I thought we were talking about what had happened in the past. Never could I have imagined that these conversations were, in fact, foreshadowing what was about to happen.

Everything Changes

Football is big in Texas.

Every fall, the season kicks off at the national, collegiate, and high school levels with an anticipation not reserved for any other sport because in Texas football isn't just about athletics, it's part of an identity. In Texas, football games are where high school, state (e.g., University of Texas vs. University of Oklahoma), and even city sports rivalries (e.g., Dallas Cowboys vs. Washington Redskins) are settled and bragging rights earned. It's where fans of winning teams spend the week after a win walking with their heads a bit higher and backs straighter, while those on the losing side slouch.

The Purpose

Games are the focal point for fans to gather and demonstrate their loyalty by wearing jerseys, outfits, and even face paint they wouldn't wear at any other time in order to scream at television screens, players on fields too far away to hear them, and, of course, the most unenlightened people of all: fans of the opposing team. I was one of those screaming loyalists.

Although I've aged since then, at the time, I was one who exemplified why *fan* was a shortened version of fanatic. Back then, I desperately wanted to believe if I wasn't watching the game or yelling my coaching advice, my team suffered. I was someone who, if my team lost on Sunday, it would take until Tuesday for me to shake it off. That was the depth of my passion. That's how much football was a part of my identity.

Today, my life is different. I appreciate great games and players, but no longer yell at the television screen, and, if my team loses, well, I just move on. However, one Sunday, during my heyday of football fandom, I decided to spend an afternoon lazily lying on the sofa, watching a game alone.

It was a few months after Susan's mom had passed. I don't remember which game I was watching, only that the outcome wasn't particularly important to me—which meant one of my teams wasn't playing. It was just one of the NFL's regularly scheduled Sunday afternoon games.

Halfway through the second quarter, while lying there, I had the undeniable and penetrating sense someone was watching me from *inside* the house. Moreover, I had the distinct feeling it was more than one person. Slowly and somewhat fearfully, I turned, looking to where I was being drawn toward—of all places, above the mantel of the fireplace. It was there that I witnessed something phenomenal.

The best way to describe what I saw is two sets of lights, which, rather than being shone on a surface, were hovering in mid-air. Later, in describing them, I realized they were reminiscent of the original *Star Trek* episodes when one of the characters was being transported or "beamed up."

During the beaming-up process, the characters' bodies would transform into yellowish-gold lights that would kind of dance and flit about, hovering, exactly where the characters had been standing. These "lights" were like that: active, moving, but composed of different colors and translucent. You could see the wall behind them. Whatever they were, these spectral phenomena weren't solid. They were ethereal.

The Purpose

The one on the right was brilliant, inviting, and multi-colored, seemingly having borrowed the most attractive blues, greens, yellows, reds, and gold from the rainbow. It was oval-shaped, elongated, and taller than the lights on the left. It was warm, comfortable, and not at all frightening.

The second set was different. It was shorter, squarer in appearance, not elongated, and most significantly, a dark, muddy brown. It was almost opaque.

Rather than being inviting and familiar, it created an unwelcoming feeling. It was colder, and although it was adjacent to the other lights, somehow it was more distant. It even seemed judgmental, as though it was assessing me.

At virtually the same instant I noticed them, I heard it. "This is the person who helped your daughter," a woman's voice said, referring to me as though one set of lights was speaking to the other.

Inside, I knew immediately what was happening. I also knew at that moment, Susan had been far more serious about taking a pill than I had ever imagined.

The Purpose

If you've never had any kind of psychic experience, of which all of us are capable, it's difficult to explain the "knowing" that comes with them. They're not just things you see or hear. Somehow, they communicate inside of you. You feel it within. There's a certainty about what is happening, one that I've never experienced otherwise.

It's somewhat like running into an old friend you haven't seen for years. In that first instant you're certain it's your friend, the recognition triggers warm feelings throughout your body that fill you from within; it's similar to that sensation. It's more than a conscious thought. It's a permeating sense and feeling.

Now, part of my certainty was recognizing that "help your daughter" referred to Susan having been serious about ending things. I knew it didn't mean anything else. I understood these "lights" were appearing because, unwittingly, I had been at a particular place and time to prevent someone from damaging her Purpose.

I was also certain that these lights were, in actuality, the female spirit who was responsible for the whispered messages I had received at different parts of my life (the brighter, multicolored lights) and the spirit of Susan's mom (the brown, darker lights), for whom, and for some reason, it was important to know who I was and what I had unknowingly done. They were there for only a second longer before disappearing, but their message was unmistakable, and the insight they provided me, unforgettable.

The lights weren't the same, and that fact would prove critical. They evoked different feelings, a difference reflected in their presence and their colors. The brilliant, attractive colors didn't just evoke warm, attractive feelings; they elicited "higher" feelings. The dark, uninviting, muddy brown lights evoked "lower" feelings. I wanted to be close to one, removed from the other.

But these were more than lights. They were alive, just not in the sense that they had physical bodies. They were sentient beings like any of us, communicating in ways any of us could feel and understand. Somehow, the conscious, emotional selves of these two personalities were able to present themselves, transcending physical boundaries.

Their appearance presented one of my most important discoveries of all. Of course, I already knew that our range of emotions is bound on one end by love and on the other by hate. The lights showed me it's not a range of emotions that exists inside each of us; it's *a hierarchical order* of emotions.

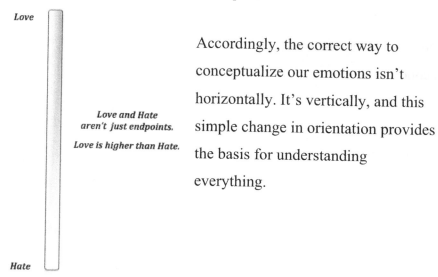

Accordingly, the correct way to conceptualize our emotions isn't horizontally. It's vertically, and this simple change in orientation provides the basis for understanding everything.

A Transcendent Bridge

I spent a considerable amount of time thinking about the lights and how they communicated with me, not just the message I received but, more importantly, the feelings that I felt. It all seemed so fantastic, so impossible.

How could it happen? It turns out there's at least one possible basis in science for the phenomena of instantaneous communication between seemingly disconnected elements, one that even confused Einstein.

It's called entanglement.

Entanglement is a component of quantum mechanics in which one particle will change its properties based on what happens to another particle even if located thousands of light years away.[7] An act as simple as observing one particle can cause another to change its properties instantaneously due to information somehow being shared between them.

Einstein's problem with this phenomenon, which he referred to as "spooky action at a distance," was simple—it violates one of his theories of the universe: that nothing can travel faster than the speed of light. As a result, Einstein was reluctant to accept entanglement. Yet recent experiments support its existence.[8]

Somehow, particles throughout our universe can connect instantaneously to one another using a mysterious communication channel that science has yet to unravel fully. The underlying physics of our universe provide a basis for a transcendent bridge, one that instantly links particles and perhaps everything, including us, across the entirety of our fourteen-billion-year existence.

---

[7] Calla Cofield, "600 Year Old Starlight Bolster's Einstein's 'Spooky Action At A Distance,'" *Space.com*, February 13, 2017.

[8] Gabriel Popkin, "China's Quantum Satellite Achieves 'Spooky Action' at Record Distance," *Science Magazine*, January 15, 2017.

But there's more.

Although Einstein may have been reluctant to accept this "spooky action," he was certain about something else, the nature of energy, stating: "Energy cannot be created or destroyed; it can only be changed from one form to another."

This statement holds important implications. It means the energy that created each of us, and which remains a part of us during our lifetime, exists after our physical existence ends, remaining in the universe *forever*.

We are created from energy that lasts forever and are connected to a universe that, through quantum entanglement, enables particles such as photons to communicate and change the states of other particles with which they are paired, instantaneously, no matter how far apart they might be. These changes can occur by simply observing one particle. This isn't conjecture about our design; this is the *science* of our design.

Therefore, since we are born from the cosmos and have descended from the stars, my next question became: To what are we connected? Are there particles within us that affect and communicate with others? Conversely, what exists out there that affects us?

Of course, science has yet to decode all the workings of our human body or our consciousness. I don't know all the mechanics of how the lights communicated with me. I only know they did.

Perhaps one day, physicists will crack the secrets of quantum mechanics and explain the inner workings of the lights and other things that may seem impossible to us today. Until then, unlike entanglement's cryptic nature, the hierarchical order of our emotions—the transcendent fingerprint for which I had been searching—is not mysterious; it's decipherable.

Balloons and Anchors:
The Hierarchy of our Emotions

Within the myriad of emotions swirling around inside us, nineteen provide the key to realizing our Purpose. Those nineteen can be categorized into two groups: Balloons, the emotions that uplift us, enabling us to fulfill our Purpose; and Anchors, those that drag us under, preventing us from realizing it.

Our nineteen core emotions are:

Balloons
Hope (and Empowering Visions)
Faith (in one's self)

Humility

Empathy

Respect

Gratitude

Introspection

— and —

Fun/Laughter

And, on the opposite end:

Anchors

Hostility

Fear

Doubt/Insecurity

Ego

Isolation (social withdrawal)

As well as the lack of Balloons:

Hopelessness (Lack of Hope)

Cruelty (Lack of Empathy)

Disrespect (Lack of Respect)

Ingratitude (Lack of Gratitude)

Disinterest/Indifference (Lack of Curiosity)

Gloom/Unhappiness (Lack of Fun/Laughter)

Their definitions, as they relate to our Purpose, are:

Hope (and Empowering Visions) is the ability to project one's self to any envisioned physical or emotional state, creating an ideal to be realized. Hope empowers us to become more than who we are currently, and for this reason, it is one of the most powerful Balloon.

Faith is the persistent application of hope. It converts dreams into work, enabling their realization.

Humility enables us to see more than ourselves, allowing us to understand the totality of our existence. For that reason, humility is foundational. Having it leads us to other Balloons.

Empathy is the ability to sense, feel, and understand the emotions of another so deeply that one becomes "infused" with the state of that person. It is a cornerstone of emotional intelligence and our Purpose.

Respect is valuing the emotional state(s) of another.

Gratitude is appreciating the respect we receive from others.

The Purpose

Introspection is the examination of our inner selves, our emotions. It expands understanding.

Fun/Laughter heals the distressed soul and is a powerful bond of social connection.

Hostility is the intense dislike of another or others.

Fear, aside from triggering the recognition of danger and a primal "fight or flight" instinct for survival, is a reluctance to grow.

Ego is double-edged, crossing both our physical and emotional selves. On a physical level, it is beneficial when it prioritizes our physical survival and compels us to fulfill our basic needs.

However, on an emotional level, it is an Anchor when it becomes excessive and drives behaviors such as self-absorption; narcissism; bullying; materialism; and more. When this occurs, ego is the antithesis of empathy, inhibiting us from seeing beyond ourselves and recognizing the greater whole to which we are connected.

For that reason, like humility, ego is also foundational. If it encumbers our emotions, it will lead us to other Anchors rather than Balloons.

Doubt/Insecurity counters hope, undermining our ability to become more.

Isolation is a social disconnection from friends, community, society, and/or other individuals.

Hopelessness is the absence of optimism and empowering visions.

Cruelty is the intentional degradation of the emotional well-being of another.

Disrespect is failing to value the emotional states of another.

Ingratitude is taking for granted and/or not appreciating the respect shown by others.

Disinterest/Indifference is the unwillingness to learn.

Gloom/Unhappiness is despair.

Balloons provide benefits, including physical rewards. Research has shown "patients with heart failure" who embraced gratitude "showed reduced inflammation, improved sleep and better moods dramatically reducing their symptoms of heart failure."[9] Individuals with hope and optimism have "reduced risk of cardiovascular death."[10]

Laughter has always been one of our greatest medicines. It can "stimulate organs, relieve stress, improve your immune system and relieve pain."[11] Conversely, Anchors create physical consequences. For example, hostile individuals are more likely to have high blood pressure and unhealthy habits such as smoking, drinking, and getting into trouble.[12]

---

[9] Positive Psychology Program, "What is Gratitude and What is its Role in Positive Psychology?" February 28, 2017, https://positivepsychologyprogram.com/gratitude-appreciation/

[10] United States. National Center for Biotechnology Information. National Library of Medicine. National Institute of Health. Clinical Practice & Epidemiology in Mental Health. *Optimism and Its Impact on Mental Health and Well-Being*, June 25, 2010, PMCID: PMC2894461

[11] Mayo Clinic Staff, "Stress relief from laughter? It's no joke," April 21, 2016, https://www.mayoclinic.org/healthy-lifestyle/stress-management/in-depth/stress-relief/art-20044456

[12] Queendom.com study, "The Nasty Side Effects of Hostility – Queendom.com's New Study Reveals How Hostile Emotions Can Breed or Feed Unhealthy Habits," March 18, 2013. https://www.prweb.com/releases/2013/3/prweb10537574.htm

The Purpose

Each day, we choose how we manage the duality of our physical and emotional selves. We are powered by our emotions, but each of us decides individually which emotions we channel into physical behaviors.

We may feel hopelessness, but we possess the conscious ability to decide whether hopelessness becomes our overriding state. We can choose to succumb to it or counter it with hope and faith. We choose whether to embrace uplifting forces or degrading ones and therefore choose whether we channel our emotions into constructive or destructive behaviors.

As love is our highest emotion, it's clear our design isn't guiding us to degrading or destructive behaviors. However, our design also leaves it to each of us to decide whether we move toward love or away from it.

We decide if we grow, regress, or meander. The fact that we are pointed in a direction but left to choose individually, the course we chart for ourselves reveals an important insight about our Purpose.

But life's design hasn't left us entirely on our own. Rather, it has provided us with a tool to guide us to higher emotions and constructive behaviors. If we operate from a base of humility, we are lead to one particular Balloon, a Balloon that is at least as powerful as hope: empathy.

Orcas

The harsh wilds of Vancouver Island can swallow a person, leaving little or no trace that someone who has become lost and unable to return was even there. Thickly forested, rocky, wet, unforgiving, and moody, Vancouver Island's rugged beauty calls to the adventurous in a voice all her own, tempting them to explore her, but the experienced know to do it respectfully.

Grizzlies, black bears, cougars, and wolves call Vancouver Island their home, but so do river otters, deer, bald eagles, and, in her surrounding waters, salmon that beckon the sea's most magnificent predators. Each summer, Johnstone Strait, off Nanaimo, is rich with orcas and has become famous for documentaries made there filming them.

On July 4, 2001, two friends, David and Kate, ventured out with me on a three-day sea-kayaking excursion hoping to get up close with these apex hunters. We weren't disappointed.

Under a warm sun and clear blue skies, we pushed off from the island's pebbled shores and into the cold waters of the strait. We were in two kayaks: David and I in one, Kate opting for a single. With three guides and a dozen others on the trip, we began the steady, synchronized paddling that would become the rhythm of our next few days.

In such a remote area, other than being on the water, I didn't have any expectations of celebrating Independence Day. However, as if on script, shortly past noon, a bald eagle chose to release herself from her perch and swoop toward us, flying directly over our heads before heading off to whatever destination she had in mind. I've always loved and have many fond memories of the Fourth of July, but that became one of my best.

We paddled half a day, enjoying the sun, conversation, and, of course, the obligatory splashing of one another in impromptu water battles. During that first leg of our journey, we came upon a fishing boat experiencing mechanical trouble.

A crewmember onboard asked one of our guides if they had a particular tool (I was too far away to hear what it was). As kayakers have limited storage space, I didn't think there was any chance we'd have what these stranded fishermen needed.

I was wrong.

The Purpose

To my surprise, our guide pulled out exactly what they needed, paddled over to them, and handed it over. A few minutes later, they were back up and running, and, out of gratitude, handed us a fabulous gift: one of the fresh salmon they had caught.

We waved our goodbyes before paddling a few more hours to reach a spot picked by our guides for camp that night. That evening, we sat around the fire laughing, sharing stories, getting to know one another, and eating some of the freshest, most delicious salmon I've ever had. It was an experience one can only have on a trip in such remote wilderness.

We went to bed exhilarated from the experiences, tired from the kayaking, and blanketed by the stars above. The next morning after stirring from our slumber and waking ourselves to coffee and cold-water dips to "shower," the strait shared with us her greatest gift. Having walked off from the camp for my "shower," I was the first to see them, about two hundred yards down shore.

"Orcas!" I yelled, pointing to the pod as they breached the surface. Everyone came running.

We got into our kayaks, and within moments we had paddled out to the center of the strait where we turned our noses, pointing them toward the approaching pod. We pulled the kayaks alongside one another, closed ranks, and formed a makeshift flotilla—as salmon isn't the only thing killer whales eat.

There was another breach, but now, they weren't the same as before. In our kayaks, we were in effect seated on the water's surface, where sound travels differently. Each breath now carried across the top of the water and went through us, reverberating. Even from sixty yards away, you didn't just hear the breach; you felt it.

Sliding effortlessly through the water, they approached us. Organized, social, and communicative, they are the wolves of the sea, beautiful, deadly, and without equal—the strait's top predators.

They continued to close. Fifty yards. Forty yards. Thirty. What would they do when they reached us? Would they divert and change course? Or would they come right for us, fearless of who and what we were?

The orcas didn't allow us time to think about those answers as, without warning, a six-foot dorsal fin surfaced immediately in front of us. Aimed directly at us like a knife blade, it sliced through the air before slipping back into the water beneath our kayaks. It was the closest and most incredible whale encounter I've ever had in my life.

Although we had considerable regard for them, it was apparent they held none for us. They continued their hunt, moving past us without concern, focusing on greater interests.

Their ascension to the top of the food chain didn't happen by chance. In fact, they may have ascended even further than that, to the top of the evolutionary chain, as the brain structure of orcas differs from other mammals.

Biologically, three different brains have evolved over time: 1) the primitive or reptilian brain (archipallium), 2) the intermediate or old mammalian brain (paleopallium), and 3) the superior or rational brain (i.e., neopallium). Human beings have all three of these cerebral elements, essentially, layered on top of each other.[13]

---

[13] Healing Arts.Org, "Limbic System: The Center of Emotions," Júlio Rocha do Amaral, M.D. and Jorge Martins de Oliveira, M.D., Ph.D. All references to the three areas of the brain as well as my interpretations and conclusions are based on the work done by Drs. Amaral and Oliveira, http://www.healing-arts.org/n-r-limbic.htm

The Purpose

The first—the reptilian brain—is devoid of a limbic system, the part of the brain perceived by scientists to be responsible for emotional behavior. Emotions, it's believed, evolved later, in the first mammalian brain.

Emotions are thought to be distinctly mammalian and absent in previous species. Admittedly, given that snakes can eat their own young, it's hard to see what we would consider to be a deep emotional connection between parent and offspring. Accordingly, behaviors in reptiles, such as aggression and killing prey, are understood to be the instinctual drives of a primitive, unemotional mind.

Although emotions seemingly appeared with the emergence of the limbic system, the evolutionary process didn't end there. After mammals acquired their emotional capabilities, they developed the ability to express them.

The superior brain, which is considered the most recent brain, enables communicative behaviors such as reading, writing, and even singing. It enables us to share our feelings with others. Writers express their emotions; readers absorb them. Singers voice their emotions; fans feel them.

The Purpose

Emotional capacity evolved as the differentiator from preceding lifeforms. Unlike early species in the evolutionary chain, we are built to communicate, share, and influence others, all through emotion.

We are designed to connect with each other.

Evolution has placed emotion not only at the center of the individual, but by extension, the center of our communities. Although emotion powers us as individuals, it is also the invisible, connective fabric tying us together, enabling us to become stronger than we are independently.

Yet evolution hasn't stopped with the three human brains, as orcas have something humans don't. Arguably, the design of the orca brain may be more advanced than our own.

Orca brains have an extra lobe absent in human brains. It's called the paralimbic region. It's hypothesized that this lobe gives members of an orca pod the ability to connect—*to empathize*—so deeply with the other pod members that the group is viewed as a single, individual entity, enabling them to work, hunt, and live in virtual unison.[14]

---

[14] Lori Marino, cetacean neuroscience professor, Emory University. This information was taken from two sources referencing material from Lori

The Purpose

In humans, empathy is a Balloon. In orcas, a physical, integrated component in their brains appears to amplify empathy so completely its members realize a communal synchronization absent in other species.

Orca pods channel cooperative behaviors. Other predators are solitary, hostile, and/or even combative amongst themselves. Orcas enjoy a differentiating, unifying distinction for one simple reason.

Empathy, magnified by their paralimbic regions, enables them to feel within themselves both the positive and negative emotional states of their other pod members. As a result, over time, their social interactions have aligned in a way to maximize constructive behaviors and minimize destructive ones within their communities.

Although recognizing the hierarchical order of emotions is important, orcas reveal that *which* emotions are channeled into physical behaviors matters even more. Constructive communities,

---

Marino: 1) *Blackfish*, directed by Gabriela Cowperthwaite (2013, Magnolia Pictures), and 2) an interview with Aviva Rupkin, "Inside the Mind of a Killer Whale," August 24, 2013, *The Raptor Lab*, https://theraptorlab.wordpress.com/2013/08/14/inside-the-mind-of-a-killer-whale-a-qa-with-the-neuroscientist-from-blackfish/

those in which each individual can enjoy a better existence, are powered by empathy and higher emotions.

We paddled more that day but didn't have another encounter while on the water. The pod would grace us with another visit later, but only after we had returned to shore, where we watched them from about fifty yards away.

We shared pictures of our encounter and talked for a while before turning in that night. Although the day had been unforgettable, our second night would be considerably different from the first.

There are many creatures in the woods of Vancouver Island. During the warm summer months, many of the island's largest land predators wait until after the sun has gone down before becoming their most active.

David and Kathy shared a tent. I was alone. After dark had fallen, but before the two of them had gone to sleep, a fearsome and uninvited visitor crept toward them. It approached carefully and stealthily until it was in front of the door flap of their tent.

Directly on the other side of that flap were Dave and Kathy, both seated upright, facing the creature as they talked. They were oblivious to its presence, even though it lurked only inches away, listening and preparing to spring upon them.

They had only a thin sheet of nylon for defense. It wasn't enough. The attack happened in an instant and caught them completely by surprise.

Furiously, I began clawing at the tent while growling as loudly as I could, sounding as much as possible like the hungriest bear on the island. Both of them screamed bloody murder. I continued for a few seconds longer before rolling on the ground, laughing hysterically.

To be honest, I wouldn't have blamed either of them if they were upset by my intended joke. But they both started laughing. Kathy even commented, "That was awesome." Instead of dividing or separating us, it brought us closer.

Fun/Laughter is a Balloon, and for the three of us during that trip, channeling this Balloon into various behaviors enabled us to bond in ways we hadn't before. But the orcas taught me an even greater lesson.

Empathy allows us *to measure the impact* of the emotions we choose to channel. In that regard, it's a mirror of our decisions, allowing us to learn the benefits and consequences we create for others and ourselves. It's this combination of empathy and learning that creates the key, the one attribute each of us needs besides love, to unlock life's remaining secrets of our Purpose.

That attribute is wisdom.

Wisdom

Throughout my life, I've had the good fortune of meeting many people who are intelligent. Yet, comparatively speaking, I have met few who are wise.

Merriam-Webster defines wisdom as the "ability to discern inner qualities and relationships." In my view, this definition is too nebulous to be useful. After all, what is meant by "inner qualities," and to what "relationships" are we referring?

A better definition, one consistent with our Purpose, is: the ability to discern both within one's self and communally the differences between higher and lower emotions (i.e., Balloons and Anchors), to channel those that create the greatest rewards (e.g., happiness), to avoid or repress those that degrade us (e.g., hostility), and to accumulate the lessons learned from doing all of the above.

The Purpose

Intellect is rooted in rational thought. Wisdom is grounded in emotional insight. The intelligent person can interpret financial statements. The wise person interprets the problems someone or a group of people is having *and is able to resolve them.*

So why do there seem to be more people who are intelligent than wise?

One reason is IQ is given to us; it's hard-wired into our genetic code. By nature, there exists a population of intelligent people. The other reason is most of us spend the majority of our time providing for ourselves—focusing on making money, getting a bigger house, etc. Intelligence enables us to realize these things, and when we encounter others doing the same, particularly those who do them well, we take note.

Wisdom, however, is acquired, and ultimately, it is something each of us chooses to realize or not. Fewer focus on doing so because its rewards aren't as obvious or immediate.

Although some are born with a more intuitive understanding of others—a higher EQ—emotional intelligence doesn't equal wisdom; it only provides the basis for it. Those with a higher EQ are not necessarily wise by default; they simply have a stronger disposition for realizing wisdom.

So why is intelligence given but not wisdom? Why does life's design grant us what we need to survive physically, but not what we need to understand everything that drives, guides, and connects us? The omission is not insignificant; it's material, and the answer is contained in the Distant Perspective I had yet to see.

My Checkpoint

In concept, stepping back from life's mural to find what I was missing sounded easy. But of course, the mural was just an analogy.

Practically speaking, I didn't know how to "step back from it" and see what the painter created. Not knowing where to turn next, the only thing I could think to do was review what I had learned to this point:

- None of us are foreign to each other. We all share a universal, emotional base that allows us to communicate regardless of who we are, where we are, or when we exist in time.

- Our emotional base is directional, pointing us toward love and away from hate.

The Purpose

- Emotions create measurable physical effects that can change us from a distance as well as through intimate one-on-one interactions.

- We realize physical rewards and consequences based on which emotions we embrace and channel.

- We are comprised of two selves: one physical, the other emotional, and to be completely healthy, we have to nourish and develop both.

- We are built with two systems of intelligence. One is measured by IQ, the other by EQ. The first guides our physical survival, the other our emotional health and survival.

- The emotions within us are ordered hierarchically, with some emotions being higher than others. This hierarchy is a universal constant, remaining the same for everyone.

- There's a basis in physics for some of our smallest particles (e.g., electrons and protons)—those with which we are built—to communicate instantly across the entire universe, transcending all previously known limits. Our physics also show that the energy that creates us goes on to live within the universe, forever.

- Within the hierarchy of our emotions, nineteen, called Balloons and Anchors, are key.

- Ego and humility are foundational Balloons and Anchors, from them, others follow. Anchors stem from a foundation of ego, Balloons from a foundation of humility.

- With humility, empathy exists, the gateway to wisdom, the key attribute each of us needs to unlock the Distant Perspective of our murals, allowing us to see and understand our Purpose.

- Wisdom isn't granted. It's acquired, and individually, we choose to acquire it or not.

In reviewing these discoveries, I realized none focused on physical elements such as our height, weight, how much money we have, the color of our eyes, etc. Instead, they were all centered on our intangible elements. Of course, I also had my experience with the lights, and they were anything but physical.

Somehow, they were all leading to a deeper part of who we are. To see that part, like the orcas, I would have to see further into us, so that's what I set out to do.

Mirrors of Ourselves

The Investment Banker

One September morning, shortly after Labor Day and before the official start of fall, the sun rose slowly over the northeast, unimpeded by even the thought of rain. The clear skies that morning welcomed her light, letting it shine fully as she ascended from the horizon, stirring New Yorkers from all walks of life to their senses and the start of their daily routines. Although New York City never truly sleeps, it was now becoming fully awake.

The energy of New York is unique. It's busy, bustling, and frenetic. Anyone, at any time, can get lost in her crowds to realize a degree of anonymity for those who seek it. Yet somehow, in the never-ending cacophony of honking cabs, aromas of soft pretzels from her street vendors, and the varying personalities of her residents, the city and her people retain a shared identity, one that's distinctly New York: proud, gritty, tough, ambitious, and compassionate.

The Purpose

For Harry Ramos, one of the thousands who worked in the city and comprised part of its dynamic mosaic, the day was like every other as he set about his work connecting businesses with those who wanted to invest in them. His morning at the May Davis Group wasn't at all unusual, until 8:48 a.m. That's when everything in his world changed.

At that moment, Harry's office shook, thunderously and seemingly tectonically. Immediately thereafter, it began filling with smoke.

The morning was September 11, 2001, and Harry Ramos' office was on the 87th floor of One World Trade Center. That day, his tower was one of four targets of massive flying bombs in the form of commercial airliners traveling in kamikaze-style attacks. Unfortunately, the flying bomb targeting Harry's building hit its mark.

Scared and confused, people started screaming. Based on the accounts of those who were there, rather than panicking Harry Ramos acted, mobilizing others—including strangers— and leading them away from the danger. Harry led his co-workers out of the office and down the smoke-filled stairs.

The Purpose

According to witnesses, Harry made sure no one was left behind, and everyone from his firm got out. As he led his colleagues down the stairs and out of harm's way, Harry encountered a stranger named Victor on the 53rd floor who was unable to move.

Like everyone else, Victor was scared and didn't want to be alone. Ignoring evacuation orders from some of New York's bravest—members of the FDNY who were heading up the stairs toward the tower's carnage—Harry chose to stay with a stranger who was unable to help himself. He instructed his co-workers to leave the building while he remained to help Victor exit the building.

All of Harry's co-workers survived.

Today, no one knows what happened to Harry or Victor. His selfless courage enabled his co-workers to go on and live their lives with their loved ones, while he lost his helping someone he didn't even know.

Harry Ramos wasn't a Good Samaritan. He was a Great Samaritan.

The Purpose

Today, Harry's loving legacy survives in the story of his courage, those of his co-workers who survived due to his actions, his two children, and his tragically widowed wife.[15]

The Charismatic Leader

Tyranny breeds corruption.

The absence of checks and balances allows those in power to dictate self-enriching policies and financial transactions at the expense of the people. Understandably, when this happens, the people's frustration at being treated unfairly can be palpable, even becoming incendiary and revolutionary.

It was against this backdrop in 1950s Cuba that one man promised to return civil liberties, democracy, and therefore a presumed fairness to all. His name was Fidel Castro.

---

[15] The details of Harry's life and experiences within the tower the morning of September 11, 2001 were compiled from the following two accounts: 1) Mary Williams Walsh, "AFTER THE ATTACKS: THE HEROES; At 8:48 a.m., Two 'Normal Guys' Met a Moment of Transformation," *New York Times*, September 16, 2001; and 2) Sal Bono, "Remembering 9/11: The Heroic Stockbroker Who Died Refusing to Leave Strangers Behind," InsideEdition.com, September 10, 2001, https://www.insideedition.com/headlines/11870-remembering-911-the-heroic-stockbroker-who-died-refusing-to-leave-strangers-behind

The Purpose

There was only one problem for the Cuban people. Castro didn't have any interest in democracy. Once he assumed power, he moved immediately to install a Stalin-esque, Marxist government complete with the torture and elimination of political opponents, nationalization of private industry, and the "fair" and "equal" redistribution of the nation's wealth.

At the time of Castro's death in 2016, per capita income in Cuba was less than $8,000/year.[16] Yet Fidel Castro's net worth was estimated to be $900 million, none of which he took with when he passed.[17] Apparently, in Castro's view, the meaning of "fair" and "equal" for all was relative.

The Systems Analyst

In February 2002, Carl Gugasian's career came to an end at the relatively young age of fifty-six. Carl was an exceptionally bright man. He graduated from the University of Pennsylvania with a master's degree in systems analysis before continuing on to

[16] Cassie Werber, "Cuba Under Fidel Castro, Charted," *Quartz*, November 26, 2016, https://qz.com/846313/fidel-castro-cuba-under-castro-by-the-numbers/
[17] The Richest, "Richest Presidents - Fidel Castro Net Worth," https://www.therichest.com/celebnetworth/politician/president/fidel-castro-net-worth/

Penn State for advanced studies in statistics. With the dawn of the computer age ahead of him, his career path held many options.

Over thirty years, Carl exercised his talents brilliantly, becoming one of the nation's foremost experts in his field. Unfortunately for many, the systems Carl chose to analyze were banks.

Carl Gugasian was one of America's most prolific bank robbers. He robbed fifty banks, stealing approximately $2 million. Nicknamed the "The Friday Night Bank Robber," he conducted his heists when he believed the banks would be full of money but have few customers. Sentenced to 115 years in a federal institution, "The Friday Night Bank Robber" was released in 2002, his term having been reduced in exchange for his cooperation in detailing for law enforcement all of his crimes, the locations of stolen money, and for producing a video on robbing banks that was subsequently used in FBI training.

With Carl's talents, he could've easily earned $2 million, if not more, over a thirty-year career in an honest field of work. So why bank robberies? For all the things Carl disclosed to law enforcement, what he didn't share was his motive. To this day, it remains a mystery.[18]

The Boy Who Worked the Cotton Mill
and the Railroad

The roots of Dunfermline, Scotland tentacle throughout the country. For hundreds of years, the town basked in its role as the nation's capital, an era that created castles in the countryside and armored knights who battled England for Scottish independence before finally coming to an end in the seventeenth century. Today, Dunfermline memorializes its royal lineage by providing the final resting place for twelve of her country's former kings and queens.

In 1835, however, the town was quite different from the days of its centuries-long reign when it welcomed its newest resident, a boy named Andrew. Andrew wasn't of noble blood.

---

[18] The accounts of Carl Gugasian's life were drawn from two sources: David J. Krajicek, "How two boys helped the FBI Find the Freddie Krueger-loving 'Friday Night Bank Robber,'" *Daily News*, September 29, 2013; and Bob Laylo, "Thief who rivals Dillinger for most bank heists is jailed ** He out-plundered the most infamous, hit vaults in the region," *The Morning Call*, December 10, 2003.

The Purpose

To the contrary, he was born to parents of humble means. His father worked a handloom weaving machine in the textiles industry, and his mother added to the family's income working two jobs.

Thirteen years later, in 1848, the economic outlook for Andrew's family turned dire, with his father losing the majority of his work. Compounding matters, Scotland itself was enduring tough times, weathering a period of starvation. In search of a better life, the family moved to America, where both Andrew and his father found work in the same cotton mill in Allegheny, PA, a growing industrial town at the time.

For seventy-two hours per week, Andrew worked as a bobbin boy in that cotton mill, shuttling between machines bringing new bobbins and gathering those that were full for the rough equivalent of $30 in today's currency. He was twelve years old when he started. Shortly thereafter, at the ripe old age of fourteen, Andrew made a career change, leaving the world of textiles behind him and embarking on a new journey with the expanding railroad industry.

Andrew's first job for the railroad was as a telegraph messenger, a role he performed well enough to earn a promotion in 1853. From there, Andrew rose rapidly within the Pennsylvania

Railroad Company, ascending to the position of superintendent in 1859.

It was a promotion that altered the course of his life.

Although Andrew had been born into a family of little means, he didn't deprive himself of an education. Andrew was an avid reader and a man of shrewd intellect. With his position in the railroad and appetite for knowledge, he recognized emerging market opportunities, and he invested in them wisely.

His investments included stock purchases in the Woodruff Sleeping Car Company (with the rail lines getting longer, trips could last for days, and inevitably, people would pay for comfortable sleeping arrangements), an oil company, and several other industrial firms (e.g., iron mills, locomotive companies).

However, he made his most profitable investment in the 1870s when he founded what became the Carnegie Steel Company. A scant thirty years after its founding, Andrew Carnegie sold his company to J. P. Morgan for $250 million. The company is worth over $7 billion today.[19]

---

[19] The reference material for Andrew Carnegie's life was compiled from a combination of online sources:

What drove Andrew Carnegie to sell his company? Was it a combination of the competitive market and economic pressures? Perhaps. But more likely it was something else, as Andrew Carnegie was marked by a rather unique characteristic—his views on wealth.

Defining these views, in 1889, Andrew Carnegie wrote *Wealth*, today referred to as the *Gospel of Wealth*. In it, he argued that the best disposition of personal fortune occurs when one gives it away while they're still living, administering where the money goes and how it is spent as opposed to willing it to one's survivors.[20] Famously, Andrew Carnegie said: "I spent the first half of my life making money and the second half of my life giving it away to do the most good and the least harm."[21]

The Editions of Encyclopedia Brittanica, "Andrew Carnegie. American Industrialist and Philanthropist," https://www.britannica.com/biography/Andrew-Carnegie; Wikipedia, the free encyclopedia, "Andrew Carnegie," https://en.wikipedia.org/wiki/Andrew Carnegie: Wikipedia, the free encyclopedia, "Robert the Bruce," https://en.wikipedia.org/wiki/Robert_the_Bruce

[20] Andrew Carnegie, "Wealth," *North American Review*, June 1889, https://www.swarthmore.edu/SocSci/rbannis1/AIH19th/Carnegie.html

[21] Quotefancy.com, "I spent the first half of my life making money and the second half giving it away to do the most good and the least harm," https://quotefancy.com/quote/1122540/Andrew-Carnegie-I-spent-the-first-half-of-my-life-making-money-and-the-second-half-of-my

The Purpose

Reflecting on these four lives, it was easy for me to see how the Balloons and Anchors these individuals chose drove their behaviors and, ultimately, defined their lifetimes.

Harry Ramos demonstrated the highest acts of love. Rather than running and abandoning others (acts that would be consistent with Anchors such as ego, lack of respect for others, lack of empathy, etc.), he instead chose:

Hope: believing he could get everyone out safely.

Empathy: not wanting to let anyone suffer or leave them behind.

Faith: in himself that he could assist everyone.

Respect: for the emotional states and well-being of others.

Humility: by not placing his survival above others.

Lack of Fear: I have no doubt Harry was afraid to some extent—he would've been inhuman if he wasn't—but he overcame whatever fear he felt and avoided the paralysis that comes with panic.

The Purpose

Lack of Ego: choosing the safety of others over his own.

Andrew Carnegie's Balloons were:

Hope: that he could overcome the hardship he knew during his life.

Faith: in himself to advance his life through hard work.

Empathy: It's hard to find a greater example of empathy than a person giving away their wealth to build libraries and other institutions of benevolence during their lifetime.

Humility: recognizing the contributions he could make to others and placing their needs above the continued expansion of his own wealth.

Although Fidel Castro espoused messages of love and empathy in his bid to capture power—Balloons that appealed to the populace he needed to win over—in truth, Anchors fueled his behaviors, including:

Ego: Castro's view of himself crossed the line into narcissism; he perceived himself to be greater than all his people.

The Purpose

Lack of Empathy: Although born into wealth, Castro had no issue depriving his fellow countrymen of knowing the comforts of financial freedom and prosperity, pilfering his nation's resources for his own fortune.

Fear: A key element to Castro maintaining his power, like that of every dictator, was having a secret police force, one that spied on its people through networks of informants. In Cuba, one never knows whether a family member, friend from school, or neighbor could be reporting one's activity and behavior.

Cruelty: The torture and killing of political opponents were common practices under Fidel's regime.

Disrespect: for his people, their freedom, their dreams, and their ability to grow.

Ingratitude: for the power and privilege the people of Cuba gave him.

As Carl Gugasian never disclosed his motive, we can never be entirely sure of the catalysts underlying his behaviors. However, even absent this disclosure, we can determine at least some of the Anchors within him:

The Purpose

Disrespect: His entire career was founded on a lack of respect for the emotional states of the bank customers, employees, and victims who were present during his robberies.

Cruelty: He shot two people in the course of his crimes.

Fear: His victims handed over the money because of coercion and the threat of the consequences if they failed to do so.

These Anchors outweighed every Balloon available to him. Rather than hoping for and having faith in building an honest life, one that could've been even more lucrative for him, he devolved into a life of crime, one that ended in his imprisonment.

Separated by geography, time, and circumstance, these men—each with two arms, two legs, and superior intelligence— appeared to travel four different paths, but upon closer examination, they traveled only two: those of virtue and iniquity. Two channeled empathy and acquired wisdom; the other two didn't.

Of course, these four men weren't the first to travel these paths, nor will they be the last. History is replete with those who have become greater by helping others as well as those who have chosen to hurt. These behaviors are timeless and universal, remaining present in our lives today.

What wasn't clear to me was why the paths any of us choose matter. What difference does it make if we acquire greater wisdom while we're here?

After all, financially speaking, Fidel lived a great life. He accumulated and enjoyed more wealth, assets, and pleasures than most people will ever know. Why should it matter if he didn't share the philanthropic views of an Andrew Carnegie?

It would only seem to matter if somehow: 1) the Balloons and Anchors we select and the corresponding paths of virtue and iniquity to which they guide us have significance in an existence greater than a single lifetime, and 2) we remain connected to the choices we make here in that greater existence. But how could that be?

How could anyone's life extend beyond the physical boundaries we know? If that were true, wouldn't we be able to see that taking place?

We can, and not surprisingly, like everything else that guides us to our Purpose, it's occurring in plain sight.

The Purpose

* * * * * * * * *

The Inequity Paradox

Several of Einstein's most important breakthroughs were derived from what he called "thought experiments." Thought experiments referenced everyday objects, such as a train being struck by lightning, to reveal how some of the most significant principles of physics—including general relativity—permeate life's design. By questioning behaviors of objects under different conditions (and applying some math), Einstein was able to illustrate seemingly bizarre but universal phenomena, such as that of an astronaut who travels away from earth near the speed of light aging at a rate different than those who remain here on earth.

In a manner similar to thought experiments, elements relating to our Purpose and which might seem hidden or impossible to prove otherwise are, in actuality, identifiable. However, seeing them doesn't involve imagining trains, lightning strikes, or astronauts. It requires only that we solve a puzzle that presents itself to each of us.

That puzzle is called The Inequity Paradox.

The Purpose

Simply, love is the force for acceptance, tolerance, and fairness. Yet life begins and exists in ways that are exceedingly unfair. If we are all God's children, and if a parent loves His or Her children equally (particularly, the One who is the most loving parent of all), why then do we begin with such inequitable starting points?

For example, some children are born into families of dynastic wealth (e.g., into the Warren Buffett family or that of Bill Gates), while others are born into abject poverty or to drug-addicted parents. Certain people receive exceptional gifts, such as an unusually high IQ, while others have lesser mental abilities. Further, some realize a life of relative ease, while others are born into pronounced hardship. How can such inequity be considered loving?

For many years, these contradictions disturbed me because the conflict between inequity and love seemed to undermine the existence of an all-loving God. Worse, the paradox became even more troubling when considering an afterlife based on a single "up" or "down" opportunity to reward virtue with eternal paradise or punish the lack thereof with eternal damnation.

For example, if I'm born into a wealthy family, one that furnishes me with the means to establish numerous charitable foundations, build hospitals, universities, etc., it would seem that I would have a relatively easy time performing many virtuous deeds throughout my life and, therefore, be rewarded for eternity. Conversely, if I'm born to a crack-addicted mother who is barely able to provide for her own survival (much less my own), most likely, I will be required to invest considerable effort simply providing for myself rather than assisting others.

Does expending the majority of my life energy providing for myself mean I will be destined for eternal punishment? What if I'm hungry and have to steal to eat? Will I be condemned for all eternity for my transgression, the transgression of ensuring I live?

How is that fair or consistent with love? Further, what happens to the infant who passes before having a chance to make any choice as to how to live?

If reaching Heaven or Hell is based on what a person exhibits in a single lifetime, that means God chooses favorites while handicapping others, a belief that runs counter to the notion of an all-loving God. For myself, these questions created a watershed moment, one that would steer me toward the confirmation of my long-held conviction—my belief in God—or force me to reject it forever. The two diverging outcomes caused me deep consternation and to wonder if somehow, unequal lives could actually be equal.

When I was young and asked questions about things I didn't understand, I was told, "God works in mysterious ways," but that didn't explain things then, nor did it later in my life. It certainly didn't resolve the Paradox, and my curiosity compelled me to discern, if I could, how it all worked.

For years, the answer eluded me. During this time, I knew only that I needed to find the resolution, even if it meant renouncing what I had always believed to be true. Since I had to admit what I had been taught didn't provide an answer, I was forced to explore two alternative possibilities that I had never considered previously.

I began exploring the first one: the atheist's argument. What if nothing exists after this life?

Although I've included a detailed analysis of the atheist's argument at the end of this book, in the interest of brevity, I'll present only the conclusion here. The atheists' argument doesn't resolve the Paradox.

The Purpose

Among other reasons, the absence of an afterlife and any associated moral consequence for how we live eliminates the need for morality and respect for one another while we're here. This is completely at odds with what we see: a world where love is the most powerful force.

I know atheists have counterarguments to this. I've heard them. In the end, none of them withstand the test of reason. If you'd like to explore these arguments further, I have included them.

Since I had to rule out the atheist view, that meant considering the only remaining possibility. What if we live more than one life?

* * * * * * * * *

"I have chosen the term 'collective' because this part of the unconscious is not individual but universal; in contrast to the personal psyche, it has contents and modes of behavior that are more or less the same everywhere and in all individuals. It is, in other words, identical in all men and thus constitutes a common psychic substrate of a suprapersonal nature which is present in every one of us."
—Carl Gustav Jung

The Purpose

* * * * * * * * *

Memory is always faulty. Emotions are always true.
—Author Unknown

* * * * * * * * *

"Nothing cannot exist forever."
—Stephen Hawking

* * * * * * * * *

Multiple Lives

This was an odd exploration for me. Although I've always believed I've been here before, the sense was a feeling, an intuition; it wasn't something I could argue logically, and, therefore, by itself, it didn't provide justification for what I was seeking.

I needed something concrete and definable that fit with what we see and experience here. So, in exploring the question of multiple lives, I sought to eliminate any personal association I might feel and investigate the notion as objectively as I could;

and on that note, I could start with one item that was completely objective: Nobody argues that life happens once.

We accept that our lives begin at conception or birth (depending on one's personal beliefs) and cease at "death." The question then becomes: "If life has the power to create this process once, why would it lack the ability to repeat it?"

Given our existence is comprised of multiple stars, galaxies, and, according to Stephen Hawking, universes (i.e., multiverse),[22] why then could there not be multiple lives? If we consider this possibility, a fascinating thing happens to the Paradox.

By returning here repeatedly, each of us is able to understand life from all perspectives, not just one. Everyone learns what it means to be wealthy, a celebrity, a professional athlete, a race car driver, CEO of a company, an astronaut, the leader of a nation, etc. We can also know the misfortunes of life that come through: the pain of drug addiction, abuse, violence, poverty,

---

[22] Ian Sample, "Stephen Hawking's Final Theory Sheds Light on the Universe," *The Guardian*, Wednesday, May 2, 2018, https://www.theguardian.com/science/2018/may/02/stephen-hawkings-final-theory-sheds-light-on-the-multiverse

suffering, and hunger. In this view, everyone learns the lessons associated with *all* experiences, not just some of them.

As unlikely as the notion of multiple lives may seem, in this scenario, life's starting points *become equal instead of unequal.* Everyone receives the *same opportunity* to expand their understanding, apply themselves, and *acquire wisdom* in an ongoing journey. The decisions we make in each life contribute to a progressive accumulation of knowledge that is used to understand a broader, universal, fourteen-billion-year existence rather than just one limited to one hundred years.

Life is no longer biased. Instead, we exist in the most democratic, loving model possible, and the Paradox is resolved in a manner that is consistent with the evidence we see here–love is the core of our lives.

Coincidentally, new research indicates the model of multiple worlds, which could contain multiple lives and even multiple versions of ourselves is gaining increasing consideration by leading physicists today. Brian Greene, professor of physics and mathematics at Columbia University and author of several books, including *The Hidden Reality: Parallel Universes and the Hidden Laws of the Cosmos*, articulates the latest views on this subject brilliantly and succinctly in his February 2012 Ted Talk, "Is Our Universe the Only Universe?"

In his talk, Greene sets forth the justification for multiple universes by illustrating: 1) problems in mathematical models regarding string theory (the notion that all particles are created by even smaller vibrating strings; 2) the small amount of dark energy in our universe, a form of energy believed to explain the ever-increasing speed at which our universe is expanding (i.e., inflationary theory); and 3) the discovery by cosmologists of an extraordinary fuel source for the Big Bang, one so efficient it not only fueled the Big Bang but countless subsequent "Bangs" can only be explained by the existence of multiple universes.[23]

One possible implication of multiple universes is that all experiences and outcomes become possible simultaneously. For example, in a parallel universe, the asteroid that killed off the dinosaurs never happens, and in another, the Portuguese colonize Australia, according to Professor Howard Wiseman, director of

---

[23] Greene, Brian, "Is Our Universe the Only Universe?" Ted Talk, February 2012, https://www.ted.com/talks/brian_greene_why_is_our_universe_fine_tuned_for_life#t-1224606

Griffith's Center for Quantum Dynamics, Griffith University, Australia.[24]

In further conceptualizations, multiple versions of ourselves could exist, each experiencing different outcomes (e.g., in one world someone might become an Olympic gold medalist, while in another that same person might fail to even qualify). If true, that would create an existence in which, on an infinite scale, everyone would acquire knowledge of all experiences, behaviors, and actions. The only difference being they might do so concurrently across universes, instead of returning consecutively to the same universe.

This research shows the physical building blocks of life may be architected in a way that makes our lives infinite rather than finite. This is important, as the Paradox is resolved only through the notion of multiple lives.

However, even though a thought experiment such as the Paradox and these new theories in physics might provide a breakthrough in perspective, like Einstein, I wanted to find data

---

[24] Michael Jacobsen, "New Quantum Theory is Out of this Parallel World," *Griffith News*, October 27, 2014, https://app.griffith.edu.au/news/2014/10/27/new-quantum-theory-is-out-of-this-parallel-world/

here in our world to support what I was exploring. I wanted information that could confirm, or at least support, the possibility that our lives continue. That meant while the physicists continue delving into the fundamental physical components of our world, I had to look to other branches of science for insight as to who those components allow us to become. It didn't take long to find what I needed.

Dr. Ian Stevenson chaired the Department of Psychiatry at the University of Virginia School of Medicine from 1957 to 1967.[25] It was during his tenure with the university that he pioneered studies into the possibility our lives transcend physical boundaries.

In 1986, Stevenson published a book titled *20 Cases Suggestive of Reincarnation*, in which he detailed his research on children who claimed experiences of previous lives. As illustration, some children could speak foreign languages to which they had never been exposed or had knowledge of places, people, and customs that they had never known in their young lives.

Although the book was thoroughly researched and documented, in the end, Stevenson himself states that his work is

---

[25] https://en.wikipedia.org/wiki/Ian_Stevenson

not conclusive, only suggestive. He reached this conclusion not because of flaws in the evidence he uncovered, but rather because he was unable to eliminate other paranormal forces that could explain the occurrences such as telepathy.

Yet, the cases presented are compelling, and Stevenson's body of work is supported by others, including one of his colleagues at the University of Virginia, Dr. Jim Tucker, who wrote *Life Before Life*, published in 2005, which documents the memories children have of previous lives.[26] Interestingly, Stevenson's work is supported further by firsthand accounts from at least one prominent figure in history.

George S. Patton, a career soldier who ascended to the rank of four-star general in World War II, talked openly about having participated in many campaigns throughout the course of world events, including battles in which he fought as a Roman legionnaire and in Russia under Napoleon. He also believed that although the end of World War II would be the end of his military career in this life, he would return to fight in future conflicts.[27]

---

[26] Wikipedia, the free encyclopedia, "Ian Stevenson," https://en.wikipedia.org/wiki/Ian_Stevenson

[27] Christopher Klein, "10 Things You May Not Know About George Patton," History.com, May 27, 2014, https://www.history.com/news/10-things-you-may-not-know-about-george-patton

However, the most interesting research of all was in the field of Near Death Experiences (NDEs), a term created by Dr. Raymond Moody, a noted psychologist, philosopher, and M.D., to describe the pattern of experiences realized by people who were pronounced clinically "dead" and came back to "life." He chronicled these stories in his book *Life After Life*, an international bestseller.

He wasn't alone in this work. Others, including Dr. Kenneth Ring, professor emeritus of psychology at the University of Connecticut, have written a number of books, including *Life at Death*, regarding Near Death Experiences.

The Near Death Experience research stands out for two reasons: 1) NDEs have characteristics experienced *universally* by people—age, marital status, religious upbringing, social status, education level, etc. are irrelevant in NDE experiences; and 2) NDE survivors report going through "life reviews," in which a person feels everything they have ever done from the perspective of those they touched.[28]

---

[28] Intuition.org, "Transcript of an interview with Dr. Raymond Moody from the Thinking Allowed, Conversations on the Leading Edge of Knowledge and Discovery with Dr. Jeffrey Mishlove," http://www.intuition.org/txt/moody.htm

For example, if someone was a loving individual, they feel the love they gave to others. If they hurt someone, they feel the pain they inflicted. In other words, a life review is an *empathy-based lesson that teaches wisdom.*

With all of this, I now had: a resolution to the Paradox, emerging views in physics indicating our lives may be infinite rather than finite, compelling and suggestive research supporting the notion of recurring lives, and even what amounts to documented stories of empathy being used in an afterlife to teach wisdom. All the pieces seemed to be fitting together, except for one thing. One obvious thing.

If lives recur, why don't we remember previous lifetimes? Although I've always had a sense that I've been here before, I don't remember anything about a previous life. If I lived one, why don't I recall it? Moreover, if life does work this way, why would it be a secret?

These questions haunted me, circling tirelessly in my mind, lacking solutions. Until it hit me—the lights. I had already been given the answer.

* * * * * * * * *

The Purpose

Our emotions are hierarchical; so were the lights. One had brilliant, attractive colors creating higher feelings. The other had non-appealing colors emanating lower, unwelcoming feelings. Neither of the lights were physical beings.

They were *emotional beings,* and that was the answer.

We do remember our past lives. However, only in some cases (e.g., Patton, the subjects of Stevenson's work) do our memories persist in the conventional sense (e.g., I lived as a merchant in the 1800s, as a soldier during an era of conquest, or a shipbuilder during the 1600s).

Instead, we remember our prior lives through our accrued wisdom: our emotional intelligence, the only part of us that transcends our physical limitations. If we have grown emotionally, given love, and ascended our emotional hierarchy, that growth— *that wisdom*—remains with us. Conversely, if we have failed to grow, that lack of growth also remains with us. If we want to validate this, we don't need our own encounter with the lights. We only need to look around us.

Every day, we interact with those who are patient, wise, and understanding, as well as those who are intolerant, hostile, and angry. We find people who help and guide us, as well as those who are interested only in helping themselves.

From saints to tyrants, we see the two endpoints of love and hate—and all the emotions in between—being channeled into behaviors by those in our lives. In short, we see people *at different positions in the hierarchy.*

Our emotional growth transcends, not our memories, for one simple reason. We don't recall that we were a merchant, a soldier, or a sailor because the physical experiences of all these existences are fleeting. Our technology, currency, languages, societies, and customs all change, and therefore, ultimately, lack relevance and meaning.

As these elements are *finite*, they can't be a part of an *infinite* Purpose. Since the wisdom we acquire (e.g., eliminating Anchors in our lives) propels us toward our Purpose, the *infinite* part of our selves—our emotional architecture—is what needs to remain intact; and a*nyone can see it at any time.* But there's something else.

That life requires each of us to understand who we are, of what we're capable, and what fulfills us most deeply (i.e., knowing love and acquiring wisdom) highlights one of the most important elements of our Purpose. We're not here to be given the answers.

We're here to find the answers.

We are responsible for our growth.

* * * * * * * * *

A Moral Compass—Even Babies Know the Difference Between Right and Wrong

David Goggins was born into poverty, prejudice, and physical abuse. He grew up in government housing, lacked a higher education, and, quite frankly, had little awaiting him besides a bleak future.

Yet David Goggins overcame the odds that were stacked against him. Battling depression and numerous setbacks, David built himself up to become the only man to complete Navy SEAL training, U.S. Army Ranger School, and Air Force Tactical Air Controller training. He has been recognized by *Outside Magazine* as the "Fittest Man Alive" and became a bestselling author, as well as a sought-after speaker on mental toughness and succeeding against overwhelming odds.[29]

Although living multiple lives resolves the inequities of life's starting points, there must also be a fair and loving reward for those who give more of themselves between life's endpoints. David's story is more than inspiring; it's phenomenal.

Yet others, who know the experiences of becoming bestselling authors, renowned speakers, and decorated military veterans, didn't have to overcome David's obstacles. That seems inconsistent. How is that fair and loving to David?

In 2012, the journal of *Psychological Science* published a study illustrating that babies understand fairness before they're two years old, suggesting this trait is innate.[30] Another study from "The Baby Lab" (Yale University's Infant Cognition Center), released in 2014, illustrates babies have an inherent sense of right and wrong.[31]

---

[29] Goggins, David, *Can't Hurt Me*, Lioncrest Publishing, 2018.
[30] Stephanie Sloane, "Babies Know What's Fair," Association of Psychological Science, February 15, 2012, https://www.psychologicalscience.org/news/releases/babies-know-whats-fair.html
[31] Susan Chun, "Are we born with a moral core? The Baby Lab says 'yes,'" CNN, February 14, 2014, https://www.cnn.com/2014/02/12/us/baby-lab-morals-ac360/index.html

The Purpose

Like our ability to recognize emotions, from our earliest days, we are imbued universally with a tool, a moral compass, to discern the difference between what is fair and unjust, loving and hateful. This only makes sense. If part of our Purpose is steering our lives toward constructive behaviors, it would be unfair if life didn't equip us with a tool, a compass, to plot our needed courses.

Where empathy allows us to measure the effect of our actions, *our moral compass allows us to align them with our hierarchy*. With it, we can follow its direction, apply ourselves, and grow, or ignore it and, by doing so, regress and succumb.

Some, like David Goggins, achieve great things, helping and empowering others to become more than who they were previously. Others travel the opposite direction, and, for the most part, the positive or negative outcomes we realize in our life correlate to the choices we make.

That truism is what told me how life is loving and fair to everyone, including David. It also told me why it matters if we adopt the philosophy of an Andrew Carnegie versus that of a Fidel Castro.

* * * * * * * * *

The Purpose

* * * * * * * * *

"A belligerent samurai, an old Japanese tale goes, once challenged a Zen master to explain the concept of Heaven and Hell. The monk replied with scorn, "You're nothing but a lout—I can't waste my time with the likes of you!"

His very honor attacked, the samurai flew into a rage and, pulling his sword from its scabbard, yelled, "I could kill you for your impertinence!"

"That," the monk calmly replied, "is Hell."

Startled at seeing the truth in what the master pointed out about the fury that had him in its grip, the samurai calmed down, sheathed his sword, and bowed, thanking the monk for the insight.

"And that," said the monk "is Heaven."

—*from Daniel Goleman, Emotional Intelligence: Why It Can Matter More Than IQ*

The Purpose

* * * * * * * * * *

*"If you can't explain it simply,
you don't understand it well enough."*
—Albert Einstein

* * * * * * * * * *

The Distant Perspective:
Seeing the Rest of the Mural

A world built on love is, by definition, fair. However, that doesn't mean its fairness is measured in a one-hundred-year existence; it only needs to be fair across its *infinite* existence.

When I was lying on the banks of the Colorado River staring at the stars, I knew that I had to understand how the universal parts of each of us connect with everything that's out there. At the time, I thought that required inverting my perspective. That belief proved to be correct.

By viewing our universe as *the center of ourselves* rather than ourselves as the center of our universe, the rest of the mural became clear; and when it did, it was easy to see life's design is strikingly simple.

The Purpose

We exist on an eternal plane of emotion.

Visually, it looks like the picture below:

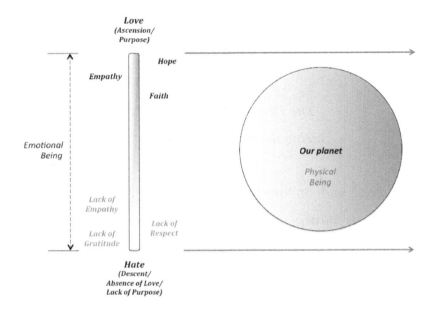

Our emotional beings—our emotional, *universal* selves—align *eternally* with the endpoints of love, hate, and all the emotions in between while transcending the fleeting, physical existences we experience while we're here. Further, the extent to which we ascend or descend the love/hate hierarchy is decided by us and is directly proportional to the Balloons and Anchors we channel into behaviors and the wisdom we acquire.

In a continuing, eternal journey of life, the path to realizing our Purpose is available to everyone, anywhere, regardless of their background, age, sex, education level, etc., making life fair and loving to all, not just a few. I now understood this was the message in the rest of the mural.

But that wasn't all, as there was something else I was able to see. By substituting two synonyms, good and evil, for love and hate, as shown below, we see what has been witnessed throughout all human history.

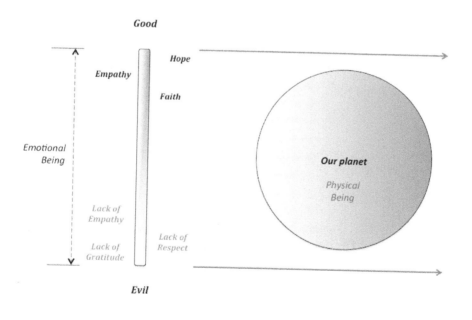

From purported miracles, acts of selfless heroism, and charity, to crimes, abuse, corruption, torture, the ravages of war, and the Holocaust, the sum total of human existence has been little more than a pendulum swinging between love/good and hate/evil, and its oscillation has been determined by one thing alone: the presence or lack of wisdom.

Taken further, another synonymous change with love and hate illustrates something many have recorded and spoken of throughout our existence:

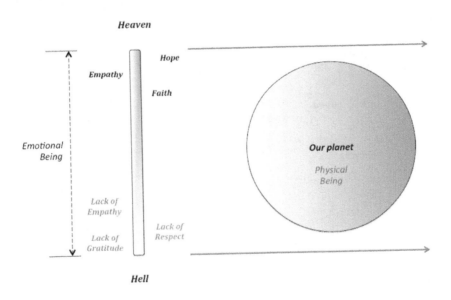

The difference here is that Heaven and Hell aren't mutually exclusive destinations or determinations. Rather, they are the endpoints of a continuum in which love/Heaven isn't decided for us, *it's decided by us,* in a design where each of us is given a practice quiz every minute of our lives: choosing Balloons or Anchors.

The mural reveals that the decisions we make as to who we become aren't binary, up or down, or limiting. To the contrary, they're infinite, limitless, and under our control. But there's still one more piece of information contained in the mural.

All paintings include the signature of their painter, and this mural isn't any different. By making another simple alteration, the painter becomes visible to everyone, at any time and from anywhere:

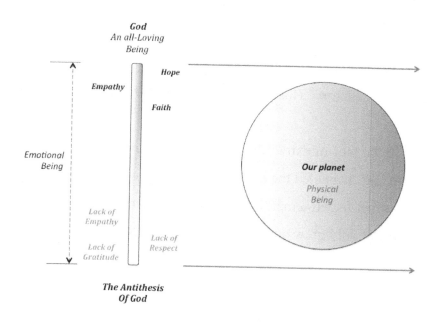

Although it may have taken a long time for me to see it, it turns out life's design isn't at all complicated.

119

The Purpose

We are here to know love, but, most importantly, we're here to *acquire the knowledge of what it is and how to give it so we can realize a better and higher eternal existence.*

Acquiring wisdom is how we do that, being empathic is how we become wise, and eschewing ego for humility is how we become empathic. Those are the steps laid before us—the ones we choose whether to take.

Our growth isn't realized through monetary or material gain. Those things contribute to how we exist here but don't chart our eternal trajectory. This is how life is fair to David Goggins.

In the face of extraordinary adversity, David didn't succumb. He channeled the Balloons of hope and faith into behaviors that fueled remarkable accomplishments, and, in so doing, he not only grew but acquired more wisdom than those who traveled easier paths.

Our trajectory is also what allowed me to understand why the difference between Harry Ramos' decisions and those of Carl Gugasian matter as well as those of Andrew Carnegie and Fidel

The Purpose

Castro. Greed, selfishness, and oppression chart lower trajectories; charity, helping others, and love chart higher ones.

We don't grow by taking. We grow by building both ourselves and, ideally, *foundations of benevolence that outlast our physical existence,* which is what Andrew Carnegie did.

However, we don't have to fund new hospitals, universities, or even charitable organizations to build these foundations. They can be built with something all of us can afford to do: teach others how to acquire wisdom so that after we're gone, others realize their Purpose, and the process continues without us.

I wrote this book because this is what I can afford. I'm not in a position to fund universities, hospitals, or charities, although I aspire to, as I have particular creations in mind that don't exist currently. Until then, in the same way as everyone else, I can share whatever wisdom I acquire out of a love for us all.

For all the questioning, observing, and pondering, in the end, it's that simple.

That is our Purpose.

The Purpose

San Diego

I no longer live in Texas.

Today, I live in San Diego where, at the end of our days, Lubna and I go to the beach to watch sunsets melt into the Pacific, painting the sky with streaks of reds, oranges, and pinks before pulling forth the deep blue curtain of night to introduce once more the stars from which we came. On many occasions, between late December and the end of February, our evenings are graced by whales swimming past us, feeding, breaching, and migrating to waters farther south in order to continue their existence.

Although they're not orcas, when I see them, I wonder what wisdom they acquire throughout their journeys. Unfortunately, I'll probably never know.

With regards to my own journey, there's more that I've discovered but haven't yet shared, as I think those insights are best saved for another time and, who knows, maybe even another existence.

The Purpose

A Closing Note—Mental Illness

There's an important element I haven't addressed but also haven't overlooked.

I realize mental illness can preclude individuals from processing our emotions in a healthy manner, and therefore can cause them to channel them into destructive behaviors. As a result, some may say mental illness undermines, or, even invalidates, an emotional hierarchy providing the foundation of our Purpose.

This is not the case.

Our bodies are biological mechanisms that are, regrettably, imperfect. They are not impervious to disease, breakdown, or failure. The hierarchy, however, is universal.

Where the two intersect may not always be perfect. We're all born with challenges, some more pronounced than others. Visual and hearing impairments; genetic predispositions to certain diseases or conditions; physical inconsistencies, such as shortened limbs or incompletely developed organs, all exist, and that's not even a complete list, but none alter the hierarchy.

Mental illness doesn't either. It only alters the way certain bodies process it, and there may be an identifiable reason as to why this would be.

For now, however, I want only to address that mental illness is something in our physical world, not in our transcendent, eternal world where our Purpose resides.

As Mentioned, The Atheists' Argument

In learning about atheistic philosophy, its underpinnings quickly became clear. Atheists base their absence of belief in God on several tenets. Some of the most prominent are listed below:

- There isn't any evidence God exists
- If there is a loving God, why is there pain and suffering?
- Why would a God allow non-believers?
- Science and God are mutually exclusive
- The existence of evil

In reviewing the above, as well as other points, it was evident one or more of the following undermined each: an ego-based view of our world, low empathy or an absence thereof, a belief that science precludes God, and linear versus expansive thinking.

Reviewing the above in order:

1. There isn't any evidence God exists.

I've laid out the evidence before us. The choice to accept or deny it is, and always has been, each of ours to make.

This tenet of atheism results from linear versus expansive thinking and low empathy or a lack thereof.

2. If there is a loving God, why is there pain and suffering?

In this argument, God is responsible for our reality and protecting us from all that exists. Unfortunately, we are not a special species immune to the effects of life or the influences of the universe/multiverse. Life's design provides us with the opportunity to grow, and growth requires overcoming hardship. Whether we do so or not is our responsibility.

This tenet results from an ego-based view and linear versus expansive thinking.

3. Why would God allow non-believers?

This is another tenet in which responsibility is placed on God for the choices we make. The more accurate question is: Why do people choose not to believe?

This tenet results from a self-centered, ego-based view.

4. Science and God are mutually exclusive.

It might just be possible that a God who created this universe, much less multiple universes, has a far deeper understanding of mathematics, physics, chemistry, biology, and astronomy than ourselves.

At a point in our existence when so many questions about the inner workings of the universe remain unanswered, how can we presume omniscience? To do so is the height of hubris.

This tenet results from a belief science precludes God and an ego-based view.

5. The existence of evil.

Evil has an important place in life's design. Without it, we fail to embrace love, and in turn, grow.

This tenet results from linear versus expansive thinking and an ego-based view.

Overall, what I found most intriguing about atheist philosophy is the definition of atheism itself. Atheists today don't define atheism as the denial of God's existence. Rather, the contemporary definition is an *absence of belief* in God.

This might seem like a minor difference, but it's material. The *absence of belief* is substantively different than an overt denial of God's existence, and that seems to create a contradiction. By not denying God, aren't atheists allowing for God's existence?

I know atheists have nuanced arguments for how they've defined their philosophy. Semantics can always be parsed. But there's a difference between intelligence and wisdom, between IQ and EQ. Atheists embrace empiricism, and that provides for intelligent examination, but it is not the basis for, nor does it equal, wisdom.

The Purpose

I began my exploration of atheism while searching for a resolution to the Paradox. In the end, I was unable to resolve the Paradox through an absence of either God or an afterlife.

I can't assure people of many things, but there is one assurance I can provide. For those who are convinced we are here to work tirelessly to fund our retirement before returning to dust, a surprise awaits.

Of course, when each of us reaches the point during which we transition to the next stage of existence, our future trajectory will have already been set by our choices here. We can acquire wisdom, become more, be constructive, and realize our Purpose or not.

The choice is ours, and our experience is proportional to the decisions we make.

The Purpose

* * * * * * * * *

"The intuitive mind is a sacred gift and the rational mind is a faithful servant.

We have created a society that honors the servant and has forgotten the gift."

-- Albert Einstein

* * * * * * * * *

Reader Feedback

Since publishing this book, many readers, including a handful of reviewers, have been kind enough to share their thoughts and reach out with questions.

Their feedback mirrors our world, illuminating delineations between those with higher states of wisdom; those acquiring it; and those who may view wisdom as unnecessary or synonymous with intelligence.

Feedback from the first group shows this book has resonated deeply, crystalizing intuitive feelings and inner senses within, to affirm what they believe or have suspected, is their reason for being. I call these individuals the Affirmers.

They are people who, on their own, have invested considerable amounts of time examining their own feelings (i.e., the Balloon of Introspection), as well as of those close to them. When they read this book, they are comforted by the connection between its insights and those they derive from their intuitive minds.

Others find the subject matter so nonsensical, comical, or somehow insulting to their intellect, they refuse to read the book or consider a rational exploration of its ideas. These individuals operate from a foundation of ego, one in which they place themselves before the universe rather than vice versa. As a result, they are the Rejectors, those for whom acquiring wisdom is not a priority and emotional intelligence is a concept that is vague, unrelatable, and/or of unclear value.

In between these two ends of the spectrum, are two groups of readers, one characterized by those who possess a persistent, substantive curiosity, are at varying levels of understanding, and who continue to explore in earnest, life and its meaning. They are the Seekers, people who feel there is more to our existence and are working to discern it.

The Purpose

The final group is also curious, but these individuals pick up the book, glance through it, read the quotes, look at the illustrations and expect all the wisdom of the universe to pop out at them instantly. They want insight but fail to realize the insight they seek is *inside of them*, not the book.

Although this book guides them to the answers they seek, they are too busy in their lives to take the time for the self-exploration necessary to discover the answers they have already been given. They are the Short-Cutters, people who will accept deeper understanding but only if it doesn't require them to invest significant amounts of time or effort.

These gradients of wisdom paint in further detail, the picture of who we are. Not surprisingly, this picture also reveals the eternal, determinant forces most responsible for shaping our respective paths: (1) the Anchor of ego; and (2) the Balloon of humility.

Affirmers and Seekers possess and exercise stronger connections to their sacred gift, what Einstein called, their intuitive mind. What I refer to as our emotional self. They recognize they are part of a greater whole and not the center of existence.

The Purpose

Their guiding life perspectives are rooted in humility and empathy for others. If given a test, these individuals will score higher in EQ as they are acquiring or have already acquired, higher degrees of wisdom.

For Rejectors and Short-Cutters, their thinking is dominated by their rational minds. That's not to say they can't or don't exhibit compassion or empathy for others.

It just means that the lens through which they view and define the world is narrower in scope, more likely to be based on ego, and less likely to reveal our inter-connectedness. As a result, these individuals are more prone to traits such as self-absorption, materialism, and narcissism, among others. If given an IQ test, these individuals can get high scores, but are less likely to do so when tested for EQ.

I have written this book so that it can be read in one or two sittings. However, comprehending its message can take years and is something that can only be realized by the reader.

As a result of reader feedback and to assist that process, I've added two items below to help in realizing our Purpose. The first is a quick, self-assessment for recognizing states of ego and humility. The second is a simple, daily reference guide.

The Purpose

Self-Assessment Guide: Ego and Humility

Are you in an ego state?

To help determine the answer, ask yourself these excellent questions Carina Wolf presented and published in Bustle on August 31, 2017.

Do you:

Value material objects above all else?

Experience considerable amounts of resentment (e.g., actively engaged in gossip, criticism, or condemnation of others?)

Hate losing to the point that you are willing to cheat or lie to avoid doing so?

Always take credit for success (and avoid blame)?

Take others for granted, feel ungrateful, and/or feel that you don't need to thank others for their help?

The Purpose

If you answered "yes" to just one of the questions above, you are in an ego state and encumbered by an Anchor.

Are you humble?

To determine that answer, ask yourself these questions provided by the powerofpositivity.com in their blog: "5 Signs You're a Truly Humble Spirit".

Do you:

Feel the need to boast about your accomplishments?

Put others before yourself?

Enjoy making others happy?

Believe life owes you?

See everyone as equal?

If you answered "yes" to questions one and four, you are in an ego state rather than one of humility. If you answered "no" to questions one and four and "yes" to the others, you are humility-based and on a meaningful path.

The Purpose Quick Reference

As a simple guide for realizing our Purpose, here are some key points to keep in mind:

- We exist on a plane of emotion.

- The plane is eternal and transcendent, permeating all boundaries (e.g., time, culture, geography, sex, education level, income level, our physical bodies, etc.).

- All human behavior is driven by emotion. However, we choose *and are responsible for*, which emotions we channel into behaviors.

- Of all the emotions, ego and humility are foundational. They determine whether we see the plane.

- Balloons and Anchors are uplifting and degrading emotions (respectively) that guide us to constructive or destructive behaviors.

- As foundational emotions, ego and humility are determinant Balloons and Anchors. From them, others follow (as illustrated in the chart below).

135

- Seeing this eternal plane of emotion is the key to recognizing our design and understanding our Purpose.

Anchors	Balloons
• Hostility	• Hope (and Empowering Visions)
• Fear	
• Doubt/Insecurity	• Faith (in one's self)
• Isolation (social withdrawal)	• Empathy
• Hopelessness (Lack of Hope)	• Respect
• Cruelty (Lack of Empathy)	
• Disrespect (Lack of Respect)	• Gratitude
• Ingratitude (Lack of Gratitude)	• Introspection
• Disinterest/Indifference (Lack of Curiosity)	• Fun/Laughter
• Gloom/Unhappiness (Lack of Fun/Laughter)	
Ego	**Humility**

- If one's foundational emotion is ego (as evidenced by behavioral traits such as narcissism; materialism; self-absorption; arrogance; selfishness; hypocrisy; bullying; hoarding of power; and/or a general disregard for the well-being of others); that individual will be blind to empathy, the basis for wisdom.

- If one's foundational emotion is humility, empathy will be intuitive, and wisdom will follow.

- Although love is imperative for a healthy life, family, and society, wisdom is the key to our Purpose.

- Wisdom provides the insight required to help others reach higher emotional states and build foundations of benevolence that outlast our physical existence. Love provides the motivation to do so.

This book and its associated website: www.thepurpose.info, detail how to incorporate these principles in order that each of us may know and enjoy the benefits of realizing our Purpose.

If you have questions, feel like you are not realizing your Purpose, are conflicted, and/or simply want to understand where you are in your journey, please come join us at: www.thepurpose.info.

I look forward to meeting you there and connecting with you personally.

Made in the USA
Monee, IL
19 September 2021